The Root
of
Rejection

Escape the Bondage of Rejection
and
Experience the Freedom of God's Acceptance

by
Joyce Meyer

WARNER
Faith

NEW YORK   BOSTON   NASHVILLE

Unless otherwise indicated, all Old Testament Scripture quotations are taken from *The Amplified Old Testament*. Copyright © 1965, 1987 from The Zondervan Corporation, Grand Rapids, Michigan. Used by permission.

Unless otherwise indicated, all New Testament Scripture quotations are taken from *The Amplified New Testament*. Copyright © 1958, 1987 by The Lockman Foundation. Used by permission.

Scripture quotations marked "KJV" are taken from the *King James Version* of the Bible.

WARNER BOOKS EDITION

Warner Faith

Time Warner Book Group
1271 Avenue of the Americas, New York, NY 10020
Visit our Web site at www.twbookmark.com.

The Warner Faith name and logo are registered trademarks of Warner Books.

Printed in the United States of America

First Warner Faith Printing: October 2002

ISBN: 978-0-446-69114-7
ISBN: 0-446-69114-3
LCCN: 2002110845

Contents

Foreword

Rejection starts as a seed planted in our lives through various things that happen to us. God said His people should become *trees of righteousness* (Isaiah 61:3, KJV). Trees have roots, and roots determine fruits! Rotten fruit comes from rotten roots, and good fruit comes from good roots. Whatever we are rooted in will determine the fruit in our lives.

Nobody goes through life totally escaping rejection; but if you are rooted in abuse, shame, guilt, rejection or a poor self-image like I was for many years, then problems begin to develop. Here is the good news — you can be delivered from the power of rejection!

All the areas of your life that are out of order can be reconciled through Jesus and the work that He has done on the cross. It happened to me, and God can do it for you. Begin to believe it! Don't settle for bondage, but be determined to be free! I pray that this book will set you on a brand-new course toward that freedom.

1

Identifying the Root of Rejection

He was despised and rejected and forsaken by men, a Man of sorrows and pains, and acquainted with grief and sickness; and like One from Whom men hide their faces He was despised, and we did not appreciate His worth or have any esteem for Him.

—Isaiah 53:3

So many people in today's world are trying to prove their worth by climbing the ladder of success. They seem to think that if they can just get a job promotion, a bigger house, a better-looking car; if they can get into the right social circles, then they will finally have worth and gain acceptance. How sad to see people caught up in the pursuit of such empty practices, never realizing that the only thing they ever truly needed was the love of Jesus Christ.

Jesus Himself did not enjoy the acceptance or approval of men while He was on earth. He was despised and rejected by men! Jesus endured all these things and more, so He could free us from the root of rejection. In my personal pursuit of freedom from the root of rejection, I have come to realize that whatever rejection Jesus endured during His life on earth and His agonizing death upon the cross was for our benefit. Jesus didn't have a problem. He was a man without sin. He didn't go through that rejection for Himself. WE were the ones with all the problems! So He willingly came and took our problems, our wounds, our hurts, even our rejections upon Himself.

But rejection is not just something the devil uses to attack Christians. Millions of people from all parts of the world suffer the pain of rejection. And a surprisingly large segment of our American society has at one time or another experienced its agony.

There are many causes of rejection: abuse (including physical, verbal, sexual, emotional), turmoil within the home, adoption, abandonment, unfaithfulness in marriage, divorce, peer rejection, etc. And there are many results. In this book, we will explore both the root causes and results of rejection, as we look at what the Bible says about overcoming rejection through the finished work of Christ upon the cross. I believe many will be set free.

A Curious Common Denominator

In his book, *Creative Suffering*[1], noted Christian physician and counselor, Paul Tournier, made some interesting observations on emotional deprivation. He relates the startling fact that a large number of the world's greatest leaders had one thing in common: they shared the experience of having been orphans. And, to my amazement, some of these super achievers had been victims of abuse, and some were severely mistreated. "This is confirmed in numerous studies of high performers," writes Tournier. "As many as three-fourths of those who become celebrated achievers are estimated to have suffered serious emotional deprivation or hardship in childhood. Because they feel so worthless inside, they will work themselves practically to death trying to have some value. And, as a result of that, many of them become successful."

A book called *The Hidden Price of Greatness*[2] relates the stories of many great men and women of God who were

---

[1] London: SCM Press, 1992.
[2] Ray Beeson and Ranelda Hunsicker (Wheaton: Tyndale Press, 1991).

used by Him in mighty ways in the past. We can learn some powerful truths by looking at the backgrounds of these individuals. The book explains how childhood suffering often sets the stage for a life of struggle. For example, David Brainerd's father died when David was only eight years old. His mother died when he was fourteen. And even though he inherited a sizable estate, he lost the parental love and affection that is so essential to a child's happiness and security.

Brainerd, like many orphaned and neglected children, felt an unusual burden of guilt — almost as if he had been responsible for his parents' deaths. The author relates that the Holy Spirit repeatedly tried to make real to David Brainerd that his sufficiency was in Christ. Apparently, he would get some insight and try to practice it for a little while, but would go right back into that "works and suffering" mentality as he tried to be perfect within himself.

God has done that same type of work in me many times, and each time my reaction has been similar to that of David Brainerd. During my times of suffering, the Holy Spirit has revealed to me the grace and mercy of God and how my perfection is only in Christ. I will enter into the rest of God, and I will go along for a period of time enjoying the victory. Then the devil will attack me again, and God will give me another, even deeper, revelation. Once the devil knows we are vulnerable at some point, he will attack there again and again to see if there is any remaining weakness he can play upon.

Do you know what happened to David Brainerd? The book says that "by the 1700s his greatest fear had come upon him." As a missionary, Brainerd died at the age of 29. Even though he had a powerful ministry, he had become an invalid — too ill to preach, teach or pray. The young man had exhausted himself, trying to serve God perfectly. He literally spent himself to the point that he became physically ill and died, simply because he felt so insecure from rejection.

How many "David Brainerds" are there in today's world, who are exhausting themselves by trying to be worth something through climbing the ladder of success? We all have available to us the one and only thing that we truly need — the love of Jesus Christ. In fact, His opinion of us is the only one that really counts!

I want everyone to like me, but I found out a long time ago that trying to make people like me is hard work! And do you know what's interesting? When I stopped caring so much about what everyone else thought of me, I discovered that not so many people thought badly of me after all. I discovered that the devil will arrange for a lot of people to dislike me as long as it bothers me! When I got to the point that it didn't bother me, those people sort of disappeared.

Rejection and the Cross

Jesus was rejected and despised, a man who understood sorrow and pain. When you experience the pain of rejection, you can identify with Jesus and draw strength and healing from Him.

Rejection is one of Satan's favorite tools to use against people. He does not wait very long to get started planting "seeds of rejection." He may have been working on you for years. Perhaps he even started planting seeds while you were in the womb — seeds to cause you to feel that you have no value and that nobody wants you.

The devil is a liar! This book will help you renew your mind according to God's Word. God says you are valuable. He has chosen you, and He has defeated the devil for you. Believe what God says about you, not what others say or what the devil says.

Although you may have been rejected by others, and even though people may still reject you from time to time, you can be delivered from the power of rejection! It may be there, but it has no power to harm you if you believe what God says and nothing else.

Rejection has no power over me now because I know who I am in Christ. I know my worth. I know that my value is not in what someone else THINKS I am, but in what I KNOW I am! I am *accepted in the beloved* (Ephesians 1:6, KJV). *If God be for* [me], *who can be against* [me]? (Romans 8:31, KJV).

A Seed, a Root, a Tree...

Rejection starts as a seed that is planted in our lives through different things that happen to us. The devil does not want to plant just a seed of rejection; he wants to plant it deep so it will develop into a root — a root that will go way down deep and have other little rootlets attached to it. Eventually these roots and rootlets will become a tree.

God said His people should become *trees of righteousness* (Isaiah 61:3, KJV). Whatever you are rooted in will determine the fruit in your life. If you are rooted in rejection, abuse, shame, guilt or a poor self-image — if you are rooted in thinking, "Something is wrong with me!" — then all these problems begin to develop in your life. You begin to think, "Well, the REAL me is not acceptable, so I need to produce a PRETEND me!"

You can actually reject yourself because someone else rejected you. Then you become full of confusion and inner turmoil. Your "tree" begins to bear the bad fruit of depression, negativism, lack of self-confidence, anger, hostility, controlling spirits, judgmentalism, chip on the shoulder, hatred and self-pity. Roots determine fruits! Rotten fruit comes from rotten roots...and good fruit comes from good roots.

If you are rooted in acceptance and love, then you will develop good things in your life — things like self-control, meekness, faithfulness, goodness, kindness, patience, peace, joy and love.

I come from an abusive background. I experienced lots of rejection, not just from one source but several. Then I was saved and began to live the Christian life. I began to go to church and try to walk with God. I began to hear good messages about how to behave as a Christian. I needed every message I heard because I had lots of problems.

Being a very determined sort of person, I would go home and try to accomplish every one of those messages in my life. I could get a certain amount of control over some of the problems those messages talked about — at least for a period of time. But, lo and behold, as I began to gain control in some areas, the bad fruit of rejection would just pop up elsewhere!

For years and years, I struggled as a believer — trying to be good...to do things right...to make my behavior acceptable. In particular, I had a very hard time getting along with other people. And if you have a root of rejection in your life, that rejection will most surely show up in your relationships with other people. It may take on many forms, but it will show up.

During that period of time, I loved God, I was born again and I believe I would have gone to heaven if I had died; but I never had any lasting victory in my life. I began to discover that I was seriously lacking a revelation of how much God loved me. Only when I began to find out how much God loved me did I begin to get well. I discovered that it takes time to recover from rejection.

The Bible teaches that we are to be uprooted, then replanted. We are not only to be replanted, but we are to become **rooted** *and* **grounded** in the love of God. We are to get rooted and grounded in Jesus Christ. Every single time you hear the Word of God, if you pay attention and do what God tells you to do, you get a little more healing. As you continue to hear the Word, you get a little more healing, a little more, and a little more.

Become a good student of the Word and let God give you the fullness of the package that Jesus died to provide for you! What is inside that package? **Righteousness** (even when you don't do everything right), **peace** that passes all understanding (even when your circumstances don't dictate peace) and **joy** unspeakable (even when you don't have anything in particular to be joyous about). This is your inheritance in Jesus Christ. You can enjoy life!

I believe God has called me to help His people walk in victory! You may be on your way to heaven, *but are you enjoying the trip?* If not, then something is desperately wrong, and God is your answer!

2

Rejection:
Causes...and Results

Almost everybody experiences some type of rejection at one time or another, and one does not have to come from an abusive background to have experienced rejection.

Recently I was getting my nails done and a woman began to tell me about an incident that happened with her four-year-old son. She said, "My little boy was so excited about being on the soccer team! He practiced and practiced! We went out to the game to see him play, and it just turned out so horrible, Joyce!"

I asked, "What happened?" She said, "Well, he was doing fine until about halfway through the game. Then this big kid came up and socked him real hard in the stomach! And my little boy doubled up and started crying. The kid said something to him, and my son ran over to the sidelines and just cried and cried. He was sobbing uncontrollably! Finally I went to him and got him to quiet down a little bit. I asked, 'Son, what happened?' And he said, 'That boy punched me in the stomach, and he told me, You're no good. You'll never learn how to play soccer. "You're not doing anything right! You get off this field and don't come back here and try to play with us anymore!"'"

She said, "I looked at him and just started crying. My husband said, 'Oh, great! Now you're crying and he's crying!'" But she said the result of this episode was that when they got home, her son said, "I'm never going back there again!"

This is a perfect example of what the devil wants to do to people. He wants other people to make fun of us. He wants to get somebody to reject us. In the world, we are often rejected unless we do everything perfectly. And none of us has the ability to be perfect, so we get hurt — we feel rejected! But, thank God, we have the answer through God and His Word! Jesus loves you, and He will never reject you (John 3:18).

Healing Takes Time...and Commitment

My husband, Dave, and I pray often about commitment, about starting something and seeing it all the way through to the end. The devil uses this issue to attack and discourage people.

When I was conducting regular monthly meetings in the St. Louis area, a lady came to me and said, "I've had so many problems in my life, and it seemed I was just not getting any better. I would come to your meetings — not regularly, but one here and one there...if everything went right with the kids...if I could get somebody to come with me — you know all the excuses the devil gives you." Apparently, she was having a hard time even deciding how to get help; then once she made the decision, committing to that plan of action.

She said, "Finally I just got so miserable that I thought I could not stand it! As I sought God, I felt He showed me that I really needed to make a commitment. So I got my mother to commit to come with me to your meetings, and we began to come on a regular basis. We sort of helped each other get here. And I cannot tell you how I've changed since I made a serious commitment to be where I needed to be on a regular basis!"

Whatever God directs you to do, you must make the commitment to obey. Wherever God tells you to be committed, that's where you must be committed. Commitment is one of the keys to victory.

Problems like rejection are deep-rooted, and receiving help is not as simple as just coming to the altar, praying a prayer, then going off and expecting everything to be different overnight. You will have to work with God toward your healing.

No, you don't have to live under the torment caused by rejection. But to receive healing, you must make a commitment — a commitment to God and to His Word. In order to do that, you must be willing to invest your time, spend money for tapes, books and a good Bible, and give yourself 100 percent to becoming a good student of the Word. If you do that, I promise that gradually, little by little, you will change!

Security vs. Insecurity

What is insecurity? An article I once read described insecurity as "a psychological disturbance that is now of epidemic proportions." A great many people in today's world are insecure. In fact, more people today may be insecure than are secure. So what happens when all of these insecure people try to have relationships with other insecure people? It creates quite a mess. It's really pretty sad.

There are some great Scriptures in the Bible, however, that promise us we can be secure through Jesus Christ. God wants you to be secure! Listen to what Paul prayed for the Church: *May Christ through your faith [actually] dwell (settle down, abide, make His permanent home) in your hearts! May you be rooted deep in love and founded securely on love* (Ephesians 3:17).

Your security does NOT depend on your pocketbook, your job, the way you look, how others respond to you or even how they treat you. Don't base your security on your education, the label inside your clothes, the car you drive or what kind of house you live in. Don't base your security on whether or not you are married, or whether or not you have children. Don't place your security in anything other than Jesus Christ and Him alone, for He is The Rock upon which you must stand. Everything else is sinking sand.

Start working with the Lord to build your security in Him. Learn how to become uprooted from all the wrong things and to be replanted in all the right things.

There was a time in my life when I was insecure. I was not rooted and grounded in the love of Christ, although I was a Christian. In fact, I was even insecure while teaching the Word of God! My security about my preaching was based on how many compliments I received at the end of my services. If I didn't receive enough compliments, I would go home and torment myself half the night...sometimes even for several days.

I was obviously not rooted and grounded in Christ, although I was preaching and teaching. I was rooted and grounded in the feedback that people gave me. Consequently, the devil could constantly play games with me and pull strings in my life to bring me torment. All he had to do was arrange for me not to get enough compliments at the end of a service. Then I was upset because I was depending on the compliments of the people, not on God.

On whom or on what are you depending? What does it take to keep you "fixed"? Does your personal sense of well-being depend on what other people do or say? When you're feeling a little bit shaky, do you start looking for someone to come in and "fix" you and make you feel stable again? We should be stable in Christ, not in compliments.

Whatever It Takes...

I don't know about you, but I have decided that, whatever it takes, I'm going to be happy until Jesus comes to get me. I have lived five decades now and spent a big part of my life being miserable. I don't intend to spend the rest of my years being miserable. If you are like I was — depending on everybody else to keep you "fixed" — you will be miserable just like I was. But if you stand on The Rock, you will find that Jesus is immovable. He's not going anywhere!

Often people in the world say, "Man, I feel like I'm between a rock and a hard place!" One day the Lord said to me, "No, they're between a hard place and a hard place. YOU are between The Rock and the hard place!"

People who don't know Jesus are going from one hard place to another hard place. They have a hard place in front of them and a hard place behind them. But when we, His people, are in that position, we have the hard place behind us and Jesus in front of us! When the hard place is in front of us, Jesus is all around us! We're the only ones who can possibly be standing between The Rock and the hard place!

Yes, it's great to be standing on The Rock! Everywhere else is *insecure*. Webster's Dictionary describes *insecure* as unstable, uncertain. When you think about it, if a person is insecure, he is also unstable and uncertain. The definition also says *insecure* means lacking confidence, unsure, shaky, and unsound. Have you ever felt that way? You don't have to!

Romans 8:35-37 says: *Who shall ever separate us from Christ's love? Shall suffering and affliction and tribulation? Or calamity and distress? Or persecution or hunger or destitution or peril or sword? Even as it is written, For Thy sake we are put to death all the day long; we are regarded and counted as sheep for the slaughter. Yet amid all these things we are more than conquerors and gain a surpassing victory through Him Who loved us.*

You are more than a conqueror when somebody mistreats you and it doesn't affect your worth or value! You may have a problem, but as long as the problem doesn't have you, you are more than a conqueror. You gain a surpassing victory. How? *Through Him Who loved us* (verse 37)! That is your victory — **the love of God**. *For I am persuaded beyond doubt (am sure) that neither death nor life, nor angels nor principalities, nor things impending and threatening nor things to come, nor powers, nor height nor depth, nor anything else in all creation will be able to separate us from the love of God which is in Christ Jesus our Lord* (verses 38,39). No matter what comes against us, let us not be separated from the love of God!

Security in Christ

Are you serving the Lord? Then here's good news for you: *...No weapon that is formed against you shall prosper, and every tongue that shall rise against you in judgment you shall show to be in the wrong. This [peace, righteousness, security, triumph over opposition] is the heritage of the servants of the Lord...* (Isaiah 54:17). You have a blood-bought right to be secure, to believe that you have worth and value, to like yourself!

The Greek word for *secure* means "having full command."[1] You have a blood-bought right to have full command. I really like that definition because people who are insecure are not in charge. The devil walks all over them and torments them. People who are insecure are constantly tormented about what people think. People who are insecure have a root of rejection in their lives. They often end up being manipulated and controlled by other people. They are "people-pleasers" rather than following the leading of the Holy Spirit. But the Greek definition of *secure* includes having full command; to be strong; to rule and to be without anxiety and free from care.[2]

---

[1]W. E. Vine, *Expository Dictionary of New Testament Words* (Old Tappan: Fleming H. Revell, 1940), Vol. III, p. 335.

[2]Based on Vine, Vol. III, pp. 335, 336.

Now look at this word of encouragement in John 3:18 — *He who believes in Him [who clings to, trusts in, relies on Him] is not judged [he who trusts in Him never comes up for judgment; for him there is no rejection, no condemnation — he incurs no damnation]; but he who does not believe (cleave to, rely on, trust in Him) is judged already....*

What does this mean? Simply that for those who believe, there is no condemnation, no rejection. We will never be defeated by condemnation and rejection if we believe. Only those who reject Christ are subject to condemnation and rejection. If you are a believer, you will find that Jesus will not reject you!

In Ephesians 1:4,5 God tells us that He actually chose us and adopted us as His children: *Even as [in His love] He chose us [actually picked us out for Himself as His own] in Christ before the foundation of the world, that we should be holy (consecrated and set apart for Him) and blameless in His sight, even above reproach, before Him in love. For He foreordained us (destined us, planned in love for us) to be adopted (revealed) as His own children through Jesus Christ, in accordance with the purpose of His will [because it pleased Him and was His kind intent].*

I like the part that says He *actually picked us out!* When the devil is on my case, I like to say to myself, "Joyce, God didn't get you accidentally! It wasn't as if He had no other choices! He looked around and said, on purpose, 'I want that one!'" It may be that one of the angels said, "Are You sure? Let me read You her background! Let me give You a little bit of insight here on the track record of Joyce Meyer! Lord, if You are trying to make a preacher today, maybe You ought to pick again!" But the Lord said, "No! I want that one! I want Joyce!"

The Bible says God chooses the weak and foolish things of the world (see 1 Corinthians 1:27). I like that term, *chooses!* God *chooses* us! We aren't forced off on Him with Him having nothing to say about it. Everyone else in the world may reject you, but God will look at you and say, "I choose you!"

Psalm 27:10 says, *Although my father and my mother have forsaken me, yet the Lord will take me up [adopt me as His child].* Did you get that? Even though my mother and my father forsake me, the Lord will take me up and adopt me as His own child!

Causes of Rejection

Just a little rejection can cause a wound to the soul that will open a door. Through that open door, the devil can bring in a spirit of rejection that will rule a person's life. There are very few people who are not seriously affected by rejection by the time they are adults. What are the causes of rejection? The list is long, so let's just cover some of the major causes. These include:

— Unwanted conception

— Contemplated or attempted abortion

— A child born as the wrong sex (i.e., parents who wish for a boy but have a girl; parents who wish for a girl but have a boy)

— A child born with defects, including learning disabilities, physical disabilities, etc.

— Comparison to another sibling

— Adoption

— Abandonment

— Death of one or both parents

— Abuse, including physical, verbal, sexual, emotional, and the withholding of love

— A parent with mental illness (the child may feel abandoned)

— Being a victim of circumstances, including extended illness following birth that requires hospitalization

— Peer rejection

— Turmoil within the home

— Marriage rejection, unfaithfulness or divorce

As I stated earlier, rejection can attack a person while he or she is still in the womb. This may be the result of an unwanted conception, or contemplated or attempted abortion. In other cases, the rejection seeds are planted at birth, as parents who were wishing for a girl discover that their new baby is a boy, or vice versa. A child born with some type of defect or disability may experience rejection, as will the child who is frequently compared to another brother or sister. Such comparison can open up a door for the spirit of rejection to rule a person's life.

Adoption, abandonment, even the death of a parent can cause rejection. As we have already discovered, David Brainerd, a great man of God, felt tremendous pressure to be perfect because both of his parents died when he was young. So abuse is not necessarily the only cause of rejection. However, it is a major cause. All types of abuse — including physical, verbal, sexual, emotional and the withholding of love — definitely plant the seeds of rejection.

A lady who worked with me in the ministry told me how she felt rejected as a result of her father becoming mentally ill when she was a young child. He was there physically, but mentally he was gone. He could not participate in normal family activities. She said, "I remember thinking, 'Why doesn't Daddy love me anymore? Why doesn't he talk to me anymore?'" Children don't always understand what's going on and may perceive unfortunate events as rejection.

Sometimes children are simply victims of circumstances, such as a newborn infant who has to stay in the hospital for two or three months before the parents can bring him home. Perhaps the doctors and nurses are not able to be the most loving care givers, and the baby senses the problems.

Perhaps a child is born into a home where there is constant turmoil. As they grow older, children assume the turmoil is their fault: "If I could just be better, then Mommy and Daddy would get along better!" While it is better for parents never to fight at all, if you do have an argument in front of your children, make certain that you go back to them later with some kind of explanation. Assure them that even though people love each other they don't always agree 100 percent and get along all the time. Assure your children that your problems are not their fault.

Often, when there is a lot of turbulence in the home, a child will end up feeling ignored. Because the parents are spending so much time dealing with their own problems, they forget to minister to the needs of the child, and the child feels rejected!

Then there are peer rejections. Everybody experiences peer rejection from time to time on different levels. Teenagers go through tremendous anxiety today just trying to be accepted. That goes for children at every stage of development. Adults feel it, too. Peer rejection occurs on every level. We all crave acceptance.

I have felt peer pressure even as a minister. Sometimes I will be among a group of ministers, and there will be some VIPs there — those regarded as being well-known. I may feel rejected if they don't seem to be interested in talking with me. Many people have the tendency (and it's wrong) to ignore or shut out other people simply because they are not quite on the same level of talent, achievement or prestige. The devil certainly takes these opportunities to inflict a sense of rejection on anyone who is insecure at all. No wonder the Bible tells us not to be a respecter of persons (Acts 10:34). Throughout the Word, the Lord tells us to treat all people alike — to love all people. We should purposely draw people in who look insecure and seem alone or uncomfortable.

There are also rejections connected with marriages, such as divorce, unfaithfulness, negative conditions in the home. All these are open doors for rejection. Maybe you saw the fruit and received rejection through a bloodline curse; and even though you hated the problems in your childhood home, you have continued the same behavior patterns. I think it's safe to say that rejection is everywhere.

Results of Rejection

If you have a root of rejection or are in the unfinished process of being healed from rejection, there is the probability that what you perceive as more rejection is really not rejection at all. You may be going through unnecessary torment — torment that will dissipate if you can just learn that those feelings you have are coming from that old root and those old ways of believing. The fear of rejection causes us to think and feel we are being rejected when often that is not the case.

Here are some major results of the root of rejection:

— Rebellion

— Anger

— Bitterness

— Guilt

— Inferiority

— Poor self-image

— Escapism, including daydreaming, drugs, alcohol, television and work

— Judgmentalism

— Poverty

— Fear of all types

— Hopelessness

— Defensiveness

— Hardness

— Distrust

— Disrespect

— Competition

— Jealousy

— Perfectionism

Rebellion is a common response to rejection. People were created and intended to be loved and accepted. So when they are misused and mistreated, they feel an inner anger that expresses itself in the form of rebellion.

Because of the abuse I experienced, I was constantly angry on the inside. I may have been smiling on the outside, but inside I was angry that I had been treated so badly. I made a decision — I'm not going to hurt anymore! People are not going to mistreat me anymore! I made some "inner vows" that nobody was ever going to push me around again!

Have you ever made any inner vows after being mistreated? Inner vows are promises we make to ourselves. Maybe you are having trouble today because of the promises you have made to yourself, such as, "I will never trust anybody again! I will never let anybody into my life again! I will never love anyone again! I won't get close to anyone! No one will ever hurt me again." You could still be living under the curse of that anger and the power of these "inner vows" you made. But, thank God, there is a way you can break free. Jesus is the Way, He said so Himself. The truth of God's Word will make you free in every area if you continue long enough to get your mind renewed. John 8:31,32 (KJV) says, *...If ye continue in my word, then are ye my disciples indeed; and ye shall know the truth, and the truth shall make you free.*

I developed a very bitter attitude and said, "I will never let anybody push me around again! Nobody will ever run my life and tell me what to do!" As a result, it took me a lot of years to learn how to be a submissive wife because I regarded a lot of the things Dave did as rejection. I perceived his efforts to take care of me as attempts to push me around and run my life. I was afraid to trust!

Many times Dave would say to me, "Joyce, why do you act like I'm attacking you?" Why? Because I had already made up my mind that everybody was attacking me! It was hard for him during those days because he was trying to love me. He was trying to do what a husband is supposed to do — give me good direction — but nobody could tell me anything. I had already made the decision that everybody was out to get me. It took time but, thank God, now I'm free!

Bitterness is another result of rejection, as is self-pity and escapism. People find many ways to escape from life's realities. Some people spend too much time daydreaming or watching television. Some alter their mood with drugs and alcohol. Others become "workaholics." But escapism never works for long.

Other results of rejection include:

— Judgmentalism

— Guilt

— Inferiority

— Poor self-image

Ironically, these traits only lead to more rejection!

Poverty can be a result of rejection. Many people live in physical poverty simply because they have a poverty image. They don't feel they're worthy of having anything, even though Jesus died so we could prosper and have our needs met. Third John 2 says, *Beloved, I pray that you may prosper in every way and [that your body] may keep well, even as [I know] your soul keeps well and prospers.*

Fears of all types are results of rejection. So are hopelessness and defensiveness. I was so defensive that if anyone even hinted that I had a flaw, I was ready to tell him how wrong he was about me, how he was misunderstanding me.

Distrust, disrespect, competition and jealousy are also destructive results of rejection. How do we adjust to all these aspects of rejection? Often we overreact through perfectionism. If we have a root of rejection, we constantly try to make adjustments for it. If we feel bad about ourselves on the inside, we attempt to do something on the outside to compensate for the problem. This fear of being rejected develops into a futile perfectionism; and we become workaholics, trying to earn our self-worth by what we do. The perfectionist feels if he can manage to be perfect, making no mistakes at all in anything, then he will never have the pain of rejection because no one could find a reason to reject him!

3

Rejection and Your Perception

If you have a root of rejection in your life, you probably have learned to respond to things in a way that God never intended. For example, if you walk into a room and someone does not give you immediate attention, you assume that all the people in the room don't like you. You feel rejected simply because you felt you didn't get attention. Now, in reality, that could be the furthest thing from the truth. It is entirely possible that the people in the room simply didn't notice that you had joined them!

I remember when one of my employees got her feelings hurt because she felt I paid more attention to the other ladies than to her at a certain event. I would never have offended her for anything! When word got back to me about how this girl felt, I went to the Lord and said, "God, she felt left out, and I didn't even see her! Why don't You cause me to see people like this girl? I don't want to hurt anyone's feelings!"

The Lord said to me, "You didn't see her because I didn't want you to see her! I hid her from you because she thinks she needs your attention, but I know that's the last thing she needs! I am trying to get her to the point that she doesn't base her worth on getting attention from other people." This taught me a great lesson — that often what we think we need is not what we need at all.

When a person with the root of rejection in his life tries to pressure us into giving him the attention or support he wants, the natural tendency is to try to give it to him. We think we're helping and blessing him. But if we're not listening to God, our response can be the last thing that person needs. In trying to give him what he needs, we may be keeping the person entrenched in his problems longer than he would have been otherwise. In order to be set free, we must let God withdraw the props. That may make him feel very shaky and uncomfortable for a season, but it is necessary...healing hurts! Real love won't relieve the pain if "going through" is going to be better in the long run.

A person with a root of rejection doesn't feel right about himself. He is operating out of an emotional deficiency. He has not learned that his worth is based on who he is in Christ, not on how other people respond to him.

One of the things I tell people in my seminars is, "Don't ever let how other people treat you determine your worth! You must grow until you are confident enough to believe that you do have worth and value. If other people do not think so, they are the ones who are in error."

That doesn't mean we don't have things wrong with us or that we don't need to change! But if all it takes for the devil to destroy our worth is to find somebody to pick on us, then we're in big trouble. There will always be those who do not like the way we do things. I repeat, **don't let someone else's opinion of you determine your worth**.

We must let God remove wrong perceptions that color our thinking, and replace them with right, godly perceptions about ourselves and others.

When I am preparing a message for a seminar or a book, I often have to experience part of what I'm studying in order to get the message. God uses my experiences and gives me more personal freedom as well as firsthand information to use in teaching. Personal experiences fire me up to share the revelation with others. Therefore, as usual, I had several unique opportunities that helped me find out how we can perceive things wrongly when we have a root of rejection!

A Tearful Lesson

One day I was in my office having a real good cry. I had been having a rough day. I had just returned from a trip and was extremely tired; it was just one of those times! I wasn't even sure what was wrong. Dave came into my office and saw that I was crying. He said, "Oh, is something wrong? Do you want to talk?" I was not ready to talk yet, so I said, "No." Part of what was wrong was that he was going out to play golf and it was too cold for me to go with him. All I had to do was stay at home and work some more. I was feeling sorry for myself because he was going to have fun and I was going to work.

Three weeks later, when Dave and I finally talked about this, he said, "Why didn't you just ask me to go do something else with you?" I did not have a good answer at the time; but after contemplation, I said, "You know, I've examined that and I can tell you two reasons why people sometimes don't expose their real needs and ask someone to meet them. Number one, we don't want to take a chance on asking and being rejected. So we just don't ask at all. And secondly, as a woman, I wanted you to perceive my need, **volunteer** to forget golf, and take me somewhere."

I knew that, more than anything, Dave wanted to play golf that day. I knew he'd rather go play golf than tromp around the shopping mall with me. But I wanted him to **want** to be with me. I wanted him to say, "Oh, honey, you're so wonderful! Let me sacrifice for you today!"

Instead, he came in and said, "Oh, you're crying. What's wrong? Is anything wrong?" And part of me was thinking, "Well, you should KNOW what's wrong!" But you know how it is when you're crying and you first get caught.

So I just said, "Well, I'm not ready to talk yet. I'll let you know when I'm ready to talk."

Dave went into the bedroom to get ready for his golf game, and when my emotions had settled, I was ready to talk. I went into the bedroom and said, "Okay, I'm calmed down now. I'm ready to talk." And he said, "Okay. Let me finish getting ready."

Dave finished dressing and came into my office. I had my speech all ready; but before I could say a word, he said, "Well, you're going to have to make it quick because I'm in a hurry!" So I said, "Well, just never mind! It's not really that important! You just go on and have a good time! I'll be fine!" He said, "Okay. I'll see you tonight when I get home."

I cried the rest of the day. I just felt crushed. All the time I was thinking, "This is stupid! I know my husband loves me! I know he wouldn't hurt me on purpose! But why do I feel so crushed?"

Well, I discovered something from this episode! Not only does God heal our emotional wounds — wounds from being rejected in the past — but He also heals our bruises! A lot of times we are touchy in certain areas because those bruises are still in the process of being healed. I have had a lot of healing, and this kind of crying episode does not happen very often. I believe this happened for two reasons — to teach me something new (give me a new level of freedom) and to fire me up for this teaching on the root of rejection.

What He showed me is that the pain of emotional rejection goes beyond our minds. It bypasses our rational thinking. I could be very reasonable and say, "I know Dave loves me and wouldn't hurt me for anything! I know...I know...I know!" But I was still crushed emotionally. I didn't understand why. This touchy feeling went on and on, then a few other things happened to add fuel to the fire. Finally, after about two or three weeks, I received a revelation on rejection that has greatly helped me; and I believe it will help you.

Dave and I finally talked about that day when he found me crying in my office. When I began to describe my feelings to Dave, he said, "You've got to be kidding! Do you know what I thought when I came into your office and found you crying? I thought you were interceding! How many times do I walk into your office and find that you have been praying, with tears running down your face? I'll say, 'Is anything wrong?' And you reply, 'No, I'm just fine. I'm just praying.' So when I came back into your office, I thought you were going to tell me something you had been praying about. And I just didn't have the time right then to go into a big, long discussion. I had no idea you were personally having a problem!" You see, what I **perceived** was not the truth at all. I perceived Dave to be unloving, cold, uncaring, and selfish; but he didn't even know I was having a problem. My fear of rejection prevented me from being truthful with him, and then I became upset. Actually, I had not communicated my problem properly.

Perceptions May Not Be Reality

How many times do we suffer unbearably because somebody doesn't give us what we think they ought to give us, and really they have no perception at all that we're in need?

Your perception is how you see things. I want to say again that many times you feel that someone is rejecting you when in reality they are not rejecting you at all. Sometimes you suffer a lot simply because of an overactive imagination.

Until a few years ago, Dave and I had a very hard time talking unless he was totally agreeing with me. By agreeing with me, he was telling me I was right, and that kept me "fixed." I needed that because when I was "fixed" or stable,

I was okay. I felt solid, sound and secure. If he didn't agree with me, I would get very emotionally upset and have all kinds of wrong reactions. I didn't understand why. Dave would even say to me, "Why do you act like I'm attacking you every time I disagree with you? Joyce, I have to be able to give my opinion! Otherwise, there is no communication! We are not really communicating if I'm only listening to what you say and responding, 'Yes, honey, yes!'" I could not give a sensible answer because I did not understand my reaction either.

Sometimes what Dave and I would be talking about was important to our relationship, and I needed to consider his opinion. But I really didn't want to discuss...I only wanted to hear him say to me, "Yes, that's right!" We are all aware that this is not communication. This is manipulation and control. As a result of my behavior, Dave lost interest in talking to me about anything meaningful. On several occasions, I angrily said to him, "We need to talk!"

He finally said, "Joyce, **we** don't talk! You talk, and I listen!" It was sad, but I really didn't know why we had this problem. I loved the Lord and was helping a lot of other people. Dave and I had a great marriage, but we couldn't communicate successfully. We didn't have wild fights because we had received a revelation on strife, and we didn't want to get into that. We needed a breakthrough. I kept crying out to God, "What is the problem?" I didn't **want** to be rebellious! I didn't **want** to become offended! I didn't **want** to get my feelings hurt! But I did!

Finally, God showed me what my problem was. He said, "Joyce, every time Dave disagrees with you, you perceive it as rejection. And, really, he is not rejecting you. He is simply not agreeing with your opinion."

You must learn to separate your opinions and ideas from the real "you." Just because people reject your opinion does not mean they are rejecting "you"! They can disagree with you and still love and respect you as a person. You must give people the privilege of disagreeing with you, or there is no basis for a good relationship.

I do want to say that proper balance in this area is very important. Some people give their opinions too often, and that's not necessary either. We don't have the right to give the whole world our opinion every time we open our mouths. That's not good for relationships either! Balance is vital in every area.

People with a root of rejection generally cannot be confronted. I had no problem confronting someone else, but I was not good at being confronted. I couldn't take what I dished out! I had a gift for laying down the truth to everybody else — "Well, you just need to face the truth!" I would say. But if someone tried to share with me about something I may not have been doing right, I couldn't handle it. I didn't know how to separate "me" from my behavior. And since much of my self-worth depended on my accomplishments, if anyone came against something I was doing, I considered it to be a personal attack. If everyone thought I was right, I felt right. My behavior in these areas prevented me from developing lasting relationships.

The Bible has a lot to say about correction, especially in Proverbs. The Scriptures tell us that a great sign of maturity is the ability to accept correction. It takes a lot of growth to get to that point, but we can actually appreciate correction when we truly know who we are in Christ. Every correction someone tries to bring may not be right, but wisdom is to be at least open to God in the situation.

I love and respect my husband, but Dave isn't always right! Sometimes I'm right! And sometimes I'm right and he doesn't listen — and he should! But there were many times when he was right and I should have listened — and I didn't! I caused myself a lot of trouble because I wouldn't listen when he was right. God gives us other people in our lives who have a different perspective than we do because we need each other. The Bible says in James 3:17 that true wisdom from above *is willing to yield to reason.* Now, Dave and I listen to each other better, and we benefit by having much better answers.

A Lesson on the Golf Course

Here is another example of how the root of rejection affects our perception. Dave and I were out playing golf. He had been having a real tough time with his golf game because of a problem with his elbow. He was playing badly that day — so bad that I was beating him! That's pretty bad! On one hole, he took three shots trying to get out of a sand trap. Dave never does that, and I felt so sorry for him!

Women just naturally have a mothering instinct, and we always want to make everything better. So when he came over to me, I said, "Oh, it will be okay." I patted him on the back and said, "You'll get a breakthrough and everything will be fine!" And he said, "Don't feel sorry for me! This is good for me! You just wait and see — when I come through this, I'm going to play better golf than I have in a long time!"

When Dave wouldn't receive my comfort, there I was — crushed again! I felt like I had collapsed inside. I asked, "God, what is this crushing feeling, and what is going on?" I believe the Lord was showing me what many people go through on a regular basis. I got really angry inside with Dave. I thought, "Oh, you are so pigheaded! You never need anyone to comfort you."

Still hurt later, as Dave and I were driving along in the golf cart, the Lord revealed something really good to me. He said, "Joyce, you were trying to give Dave what you would need in that situation! But he doesn't need it, so he didn't receive it. Since you need that kind of comfort when you are having a hard time, you feel rejected because he isn't receiving it from you."

The more I thought about that, the more revelation I received! I think people do that sort of thing all the time in relationships; they try to give other people what they need themselves. But the other person rejects it because he doesn't really need it; he is not doing that on purpose. It would be no different than having a glass of water offered to you and rejecting it because you were not thirsty. A rejection-based person can't understand how anybody who loved him could reject his comfort, because if somebody would just give it to him, he would be delighted!

Are you trying to give people what you need, and then feeling rejected if they don't want it? When I shop for a present for someone, I find that I want to buy them what I like. But now, I try to think of what they would really like. Sometimes, people buy me things that are just not "me" at all, and I wonder why in the world they would buy me something like that. But now I have the answer. We try to give to others what we would want. I believe this truth is going to help in many relationships. It has certainly helped me, and I pray it will help you.

A Lesson at the Post Office

The next little lesson occurred one day when Dave and I went to the post office. I like for people to pay attention to me when I'm talking to them. Maybe that's the teacher in me. Dave had just come out of the post office, and I was talking to him about something that I considered to be pretty important. It was important to ME! Dave is one of those "detail" people who gets caught up in things I don't even see. So there we were — I was in this intense conversation, and all of a sudden I realize that Dave doesn't seem to be listening to me. He said, "Oh, look at that man coming out of the post office! His shirt is ripped all the way down the back!"

I said, "Dave, I am trying to talk to you about something important." And he said, "Well, I just wanted you to look at that man's shirt!" I felt he was more interested in the man's ripped shirt than me.

Again I felt that crushing rejection. And the whole episode was simply due to the difference in our personalities. Dave was not trying to be rude to me. It was just that something caught his eye and drew his attention. It happened to be something I didn't care about, so I couldn't imagine how he could ignore my great conversation in favor of watching a man whose shirt was ripped! Once again I perceived it as rejection. My perception was wrong; still affected, or perhaps I should say *infected*, by the root of rejection in my life.

It's interesting how different we think when we are looking at things through a lifetime of dealing with rejection. I don't believe I have this big root of rejection any longer — I've had a lot of major deliverance. But I have found that any time a person has been sick in a particular area — whether emotional or physical — there will be a little tenderness in those areas, a bruise. Sometimes for a long time even after the person receives healing, he will be a little touchy in those areas. If this describes you, do not be discouraged. Let each incident be a learning experience — and then you can be propelled forward — not dragged backward.

Testing the Revelation

Dave and I were planning to be out of town on Mother's Day. My son David called and invited me out to dinner. He asked, "Are you doing anything on Monday night?" I said, "No." And he said, "Well, your four children are going to take you out to dinner for Mother's Day, since you're not going to be in town on Sunday. It's going to be just you and your four children. Dad is not invited, and none of our spouses are invited."

Immediately I said, "You're not going to ask your father?" He said, "No — he's not our mother! We thought this would be something different — something special. Usually when we're with you, everybody is there — all the grandchildren, all the spouses, Dad, everybody. We thought it would be nice for you to go out and have a meal with just your four kids."

I thought, "Well, yeah, that would be nice!" Then I said, "But we don't want to hurt your father's feelings...we don't want to insult him!"

My son asked, "Oh, do you think he'll get his feelings hurt? I'm not trying to hurt anybody! If you think it will bother Dad, go ahead and invite him. But I don't think Dad's feelings will be hurt."

I began to think about it and realized that I was responding to the situation according to the way I would feel if the kids asked Dave out for dinner and did not invite me. This was a real eye-opener for me! I realized that many times we respond to other people based on what we ourselves need. I could just imagine how I would feel if the children said, "We're going to take Dad out." I would say, "Well, where are **we** going?" And the children would say, "Well, actually, Mom, we're not taking you. We're just taking Dad!"

"You're not taking **me**! Well, what's wrong with **me**? What have you got against **me**?"

Again my son said, "I really cannot imagine Dad feeling rejected if we don't take him out for Mother's Day, but you do what you think is best."

So I thought, "Okay, I'm going to test this." I went to Dave and said, "The children are going to take me out for Mother's Day — just the four of them and me. What do you think?" He said, "Oh, I think that's a great idea! I'll go out to the driving range and hit golf balls!"

My husband is so secure! Just recently Dave and I talked about that. I said, "Dave, you have no idea how blessed you are to be so secure." He doesn't care what anybody thinks! It would never occur to him that his children were rejecting him because they asked me out to dinner and did not ask him.

I asked, "What was your first thought when I told you the children had invited me out for dinner and had not invited you?" He said, "Well, I thought that was a real unique, creative idea. I thought, 'That will be really good for Joyce to go out with the kids. I'll just take advantage of that and go out and hit some golf balls and get a bite to eat with one of the guys.'" He just thought it was great!

Before I close this section, always remember to check your perception when you feel rejected. Just because you **feel** rejected or **perceive** rejection doesn't mean you are really being rejected. It may be the result of past problems; and, if so, it is time to receive healing.

4
Walls of Protection

The pain of emotional rejection is one of the worst kinds of pain a person can feel. When a person feels he has been rejected, there is intense emotional pain! It hurts!

I believe we work harder to avoid emotional pain than we do physical pain. Therefore, we build many elaborate defense systems to protect our emotions from the pain of rejection. Self-made walls are one such defense system. We put up an invisible (but real) wall between us and anyone who might be able to hurt us.

One sweet girl wrote me a letter recently and said that attending my seminars had changed her life. She said God really ministered to her one night when I taught about walls. She said, "I realized that for years I've been trying to keep people out of my life simply because I was afraid of rejection. I would see somebody I knew in a grocery store, but I would pretend not to see her and hurry to get away from her. I was afraid if I said something to her that she might reject me! Then I would have to deal with the pain of rejection!"

You see, Satan works in many different ways to steal your freedom and your joy. These two go together! If Satan steals your freedom, he will also steal your joy. You will end up living in a little box, always trying to do what you think will be acceptable to everybody else...never being led by the Holy Spirit within you.

The Meaning of Rejection

The word *rejection* means to be cast aside; to be thrown away as having no value. To be rejected means being told,

"I don't want you — you have no value! You're not what I want! You're not right!" When that happens to a person, it is very painful. God did not create us to be rejected. He created us to be accepted, loved and valuable. There is nothing in our God-given nature that can accept being rejected.

The Bible teaches us in Ephesians, chapter 1, that we have been *accepted in the beloved* (verse 6, KJV). We never have to worry about whether or not we are acceptable to God. If we believe in Jesus and receive Him as our Savior, there is always one Person Who will never reject us. He doesn't demand that we shape up and become perfect before He will accept us. There is healing in just knowing that Jesus offers us unconditional love.

Multiplied millions of people on earth today are receiving healing from the wounds of rejection through a personal relationship with Jesus Christ. You can't get that anywhere else. No matter how many classes you go to or how many self-help books you read, I don't believe you can be permanently healed from the wounds of abuse and rejection without a personal, vital relationship with the Lord Jesus Christ.

Rejection attacks everyone. I don't believe there is anyone anywhere who has not at some time been attacked by the devil with rejection. You were fortunate if you had parents who really knew the Word of God and knew how to teach you about your value apart from what you did and apart from what other people thought of you. Or if you have the kind of personality that is not extremely sensitive, and you are able to cast your care upon the Lord and throw things off easier, that's also to your advantage. With these advantages, the devil's rejection attacks may have hurt you less severely than others. But there are very few people who fall into this category.

Rejection by Inheritance

Most people were raised by parents who, although they did the best they could, already had a root of rejection in their lives. They didn't know what to do except pass it on to their children. Most people don't know how to separate a person's "who" from their "do." A child spills a glass of milk and the parent says, "Bad boy! Bad girl!" The child has no choice but to think that every time they *do* something bad, they *are* bad.

Many of us have done that to our children — I know I did. Thank God, I knew the Word by the time I had my last child, so he hasn't spent his entire life hearing how bad he is. We've been able to tell him, "What you did was bad, but you are good; deep down inside, you're wonderful! You are great, and God will help you bring out your best. We're committed to love you no matter what."

It's great when parents instill that godly confidence in their children, but not everybody is that fortunate. Most of the people we deal with in everyday life are people who have roots of rejection. Rejected people are trying to have relationships with other rejected people. Consequently, nobody is operating normally the way they should, and multitudes are continuing to be hurt. ***Hurting people hurt people.***

God's Part and Our Part

When we are busy trying to change someone — friends, family, even ourselves — God is not going to work. He works through faith, which is dependence upon Him...not works of the flesh, which is independence. He will not become involved until we get our hands off the situation and turn it over to Him. Have you learned that? You will frustrate yourself unbearably until you learn that you are not to try to do the work of the Holy Spirit! You can't take on the job of making all the necessary changes in your life. That's not your job — it's the job of the Holy Spirit!

When we try to do God's job, we don't make progress; and we become frustrated. When we let God do His job in our lives, we make progress. So we really need to learn to do our part and let God do His part. Most of the time, however, we are so busy trying to do God's part that we don't do our part! Our part is to believe; His part is to do.

God wants to build His walls of protection around us, but as long as we are trying to do His job — as long as we are trying to protect ourselves — God doesn't do it. As God's children, we don't have to labor to protect ourselves. We should place our faith in His protection. If we continue trying to do it ourselves, we may find that we are not protected at all. We can spend so much time trying to protect ourselves from the pain of rejection that we never build a healthy, loving, balanced relationship. But if we allow the Holy Spirit to tear down the wrong walls, then He can activate the protection of God that became available to us through salvation.

I want to clarify something regarding God's protection. I'm not going to tell you that, if you trust God, you'll never be rejected! Isaiah 53:3 (KJV) says Jesus was despised and rejected of men. **He was forsaken.** I believe that anything Jesus endured He endured for me — either so I would never have to go through it, or so I could go through it victoriously. We must look at both of those aspects of the work of Christ upon the cross.

Sometimes I can pray and avoid rejection. Sometimes I can pray; and while I may still have to experience rejection, I can go through it victoriously without being devastated by it. So I think it would be off base to say that you can live your life without ever being rejected again. I don't really think that's possible because rejection is a frequently used attack of the enemy.

The devil loves to use rejection to keep people from feeling right about themselves and having victory. He also uses rejection to keep people from simply obeying God or to keep them from going forward. Many people won't step out. They never get out of the boat, so to speak. They would love to "walk on water," but fear of rejection keeps them in the boat all their lives. They protect themselves from the possibility of rejection or failure by always staying in "the safety zone." God wants to set us free from fear and help us.

When people hurt you, do you erect walls? I know I do! Dave and I have a good marriage. We've been married over twenty-seven years, and we have four children. But when Dave hurts me, I can feel it in my emotions. God wants to teach us how to handle those situations His way and not our way.

By Faith

Every time you sense a wall going up, you must choose to bring it down — by faith! As God continues to reveal to you the walls in your life, you must bring each one of them down — by faith! Let Jesus help you tear down the self-made walls so He can become a wall of protection to you.

Hebrews 11 is called the great faith chapter of the Bible. In it we are told that the heroes of the Bible accomplished great things for God by faith. By faith, Noah built the ark...by faith, Abraham believed God for a son...by faith, Sarah had a child in her old age. Hebrews 11:30 (KJV) says, *By faith the walls of Jericho fell down....* Everything was accomplished by faith! Faith acts on God's Word, and then sees.

When a person gets hurt, right away his mind says, "You're not going to hurt me again!" — and up goes a wall! I've learned that when Dave hurts me and I feel a wall going up, I have to tear that wall down by faith. I say, "Okay, God, I feel a wall going up! Help me to tear it down

45

by faith!" Instead of taking care of myself, I trust God to do it.

Another thing I've discovered is that I cannot give and receive love as long as there is a wall between me and another individual. And since love is the key to all victorious Christianity, how can I flow in the love of God if I have walls up around me? Why are the walls there? Because I was afraid of being hurt. But I finally realized that I was getting hurt anyway. Living behind walls is also painful. If I let the walls down, and Dave hurts me again next week (which he may), I have still had the opportunity and freedom to give and receive love this week. If I live behind walls, I'm hurting all the time. If, by faith, I tear them down and open my life up to others, I may get hurt occasionally; but that is better than living an isolated, lonely life all the time.

When you have walls up, you are miserable! It definitely takes a step of faith for you to let down those walls you've lived behind for so many years. But when you do, it will be a whole new way of living! You will be like a prisoner who has been pardoned from jail. You may not know quite how to act as you come out from behind those walls. You'll have to take a chance on being hurt again.

"I'm afraid!" you say. The Bible says, *God hath not given us the spirit of fear; but of power, and of love, and of a sound mind* (2 Timothy 1:7, KJV). So if you're keeping those walls up out of fear, you're not living God's way. Yes, taking down your walls may mean that you'll get hurt, but I have wonderful news: the Healer and Comforter lives on the inside of you (if you're born again), and He can heal your hurts.

I have no promise that Dave will never hurt me again. There is no promise that my children will never hurt me again or that I won't hurt them. But there is a promise that some way, somehow, God will make it all right if I place my trust in Him.

Staying in a relationship — whether it be marriage, friendship or a dating relationship — and keeping those walls up all the time is not God's way of relating.

Isaiah 26:1 says, *In that day shall this song be sung in the land of Judah: We have a strong city; [the Lord] sets up salvation as walls and bulwarks.* A footnote in *The Amplified Bible* says, "*The Dead Sea Scrolls* read, 'You [Lord] have been to me a strong wall.'" God wants to be your wall! *You will guard him and keep him in perfect and constant peace whose mind [both its inclination and its character] is stayed on You, because he commits himself to You, leans on You, and hopes confidently in You. So trust in the Lord (commit yourself to Him, lean on Him, hope confidently in Him) forever; for the Lord God is an everlasting Rock [the Rock of Ages]* (verses 3,4). **Wow!**

Do you know what God is saying in these verses? Ask yourself, "Do I have the peace I should have as part of my covenant?" If you want that peace but are not experiencing it, perhaps it is because you are trying to take care of yourself instead of letting God take care of you! Let some of those wrong walls come down through trusting God, and then you'll receive His peace. Even if you remain in the midst of turmoil for a season while God is turning your situation around, trusting Him brings "peace in the midst of the storm."

Sometimes we feel like God just forgets us in the midst of our hurts, but this is a lie of the devil! Isaiah 49:15,16 says: *[And the Lord answered] Can a woman forget her nursing child, that she should not have compassion on the son of her womb? Yes, they may forget, yet I will not forget you. Behold, I have indelibly imprinted (tattooed a picture of) you on the palm of each of My hands; [O Zion] your walls are continually before me.* God is continually concerned about our protection. Not only can we trust Him with our physical protection, but our emotional protection as well.

Dave and I recognized the protection of God recently when we were out of town. We pulled into a drive-in restaurant, and Dave went inside to place our order. I was sitting in the car, minding my own business, when a car rammed into the back of our car! It was a pretty hard impact, but there was no damage to our car.

A few minutes later, as we were preparing to pull out of the parking lot and into the traffic, another car zoomed in front of us and came within three hairs of hitting us. Thank God for the Word! I said, "I rebuke the spirit of accidents, in the name of Jesus!" I believe there are certain powers and principalities over certain areas. Those close calls were attacks from the devil! You don't get hit going in...and almost get hit going out! But in both instances, God protected us.

It's easy to understand God's physical protection. You can see God's hand in your life when you almost have an accident; and, miraculously, it doesn't happen. But God wants us to go beyond what we can see with our natural eye and begin to believe Him for emotional protection. We can only receive God's emotional protection by faith! He wants us to exercise our faith and tear down those walls we have built up inside.

Trust God for Emotional Protection!

You say, "Well, I'm going to do this because it's in the Word. I love God, so I'm going to do it! But I'm so afraid!" I understand how you feel, but it is important that you press through to victory. Just as you believe God for physical protection on a regular basis, you can start believing Him to protect you emotionally.

Don't wait until you're hurt or devastated to start believing. Believe God for emotional protection on a regular basis. Every day when you go out among people, you can say, "God, I'm believing You to protect me emotionally. I'm not going to have those walls up anymore! I'm trusting You to protect me from emotional rejection!"

If we are trusting God instead of living in fear, we won't be devastated by rejection. Even when it comes, we'll hardly be affected by it at all.

Don't go to work with all your walls up. Don't dwell on thoughts like, "These people said this, so I'm not letting them in anymore! I see them; but I'm going to act like I don't, because I don't want to deal with their rejection. I'm going to get over there in a corner and eat lunch by myself because they reject my Christianity. And I'm not going to ask them how they like my new hairdo because if they don't like it, I'll feel rejected!

Isn't that a pitiful way to live? God doesn't want you to live that way. You need to be able to come out of your house and say, "I'm the King's kid! I'm not like everybody else; but, praise God, I'm me! And I'm going to walk out of this place today in faith! I'm going out without my walls! I'm being brave! I'm believing God today."

Believe me, this is going to take faith! It takes faith to say, "I'm going out without my walls, and I'm trusting You, God! I'm going out in faith! I'm tearing my walls down by faith, and I'm asking for Your walls to be activated in my life." But it is well worth the effort!

5
Rejection Protection Patterns

Rejection Protection Pattern #1: Inner Vows

Some of the major building blocks of our own walls of protection are inner vows. These are promises we make to ourselves to protect ourselves. Here are some examples:

— Nobody will ever hurt me again!

— When I get out of this situation, nobody will ever push me around again!

— I'll never let anyone get close enough to hurt me again!

— Nobody is ever going to control me again!

— I'm going to run my own life from now on — nobody will ever tell me what to do again!

We make promises like these to ourselves not just once — but over and over again. We tell ourselves these things on the inside. While growing up for fifteen years in an abusive home, how many times do you think I said, "When I get out of here, nobody will ever push me around again!" No wonder it took an act of God to teach me how to be submissive to authority!

Walls Create Blockages

People in prayer lines often tell me, "I'm fine in every kind of relationship except an intimate relationship. I just can't get into any kind of close, intimate relationship; something is wrong — there is some kind of blockage. I date, and I'm just fine until it starts to look like it could turn into a permanent thing. I don't know what my problem is; but at that point I start backing off, even though I don't want to."

This problem is usually the result of walls built through inner vows — saying over and over, "Nobody is ever going to get close enough to me again to hurt me!"

Or how about this one: "Nobody is ever going to control me again! I'll run my own life from now on, and never again will anybody ever tell me what to do!" I had grooves worn on the inside of me from saying that one over and over.

People can make inner vows concerning many things. Consider this...many people are in bondage today because their parents were out of balance on one issue or another. For instance, I went through a period in my life when I was trying to teach my children to eat right. I wouldn't let them have any sugar. I would say, "You're not going to eat that stuff!" I probably went a bit overboard, which many of us do until we learn more about balance. Now I realize that it would have been better if I had let them have some sugar occasionally, but I made a *law* of not eating it, which only made them want it more. I don't have a problem with sugar — I can eat two bites of something sweet and be satisfied. But my children are not that way — they love sugar and think they just have to have it!

We have talked about why they all like sugar so well, and I wonder if it might be because they were not allowed to have it at all as children.

Situations like this can cause children to vow, "When I get out of here, I bet you I'll eat everything I can get my hands on, and nobody will ever tell me again that I cannot eat something!" And many of those individuals develop eating disorders later in life because they've made all these promises to themselves.

God even wants to get involved in your appetite! Did you know that, if you have built walls, it may be difficult to listen even when God is talking to you? But as your relationship with God grows and you get more of the Word inside you, He will begin to deal with you about your appetite. He'll say, "I don't want you to eat like that anymore!"

Money may be an area where you have built a wall. Maybe your parents wouldn't give you much money to spend when you were younger, and you had to do without some things other children had. Maybe the only money you could spend was what you managed to earn and save. And maybe even then you had to purchase only things you really needed and weren't allowed to buy the things you wanted. Perhaps you got so tired of having no financial liberty that you began promising yourself, "Just wait until I get out of here! I'll buy anything I want, anytime I want it!"

A shopping addiction could result from inner vows like these. There are people who are addicted to shopping — they just can't stop spending money!

Maybe you need to think about some of those things you said to yourself over and over, a long time ago. I'm not saying that everything you say to yourself creates a bondage in your life. I am talking specifically about things we say that involve definite, determined agreements with ourselves. These inner vows are decisions we make concerning how we will take care of and protect ourselves.

How about this one? "You can't trust anybody!" Oh, how many times I said that! "You can't trust men! All men are alike!" I don't mean to be crude, but I think that some women have trouble when they marry — even in their sex lives — because they say things to themselves like, "All men are just out for one thing!" Even in a marriage relationship, when you want things to be right, you may think to yourself, "You don't really love me! The only time you show me any affection is when you want sex!" Be careful of wrong self-talk.

Walls Prevent Involvement

Wrong systems of thinking can also cause us to draw back from involvement in groups of people. Because of some hurt or rejection, we may say, "I will never get involved with a group of people again!" So we withdraw and isolate ourselves.

I was hurt very badly several years ago by a group of Christians — I mean it was bad! I've never had to deal with emotional pain like that! I trusted those people more than I trusted anybody, and it took me almost three years to totally get over the hurt. I had these big walls up, and I was firm: **Nobody is ever going to get in a position to do that to me again!** That is not God's plan for your church life. Every member should be involved.

God gave me a really great example of what it means to be involved in church. One day I stepped on my own foot and it hurt! I yanked my foot up right away; and while I was holding it, God spoke to me: "Now, Joyce, notice that even though you stepped on your own foot and it hurt, immediately you withdrew that member because you didn't want it to get hurt again. But eventually, in order for that foot to be part of the body, you must put that foot back down and take a chance on stepping on it again!" I could not walk properly until I got my hurt foot involved again.

If someone in your church or family hurts you, the immediate reaction is to withdraw. The Lord showed me that never getting involved again is like hobbling around all your life on one foot. You cripple yourself by your own choice, simply by saying, "Oh, that hurts! I'm not going to let that happen again!" You put up a wall and withdraw behind it!

Rejection Protection Pattern #2: Pretense

In addition to trying to protect myself from rejection through inner vows, I also pretended that I didn't care! **You can't hurt me because I don't care!**

Someone may ask, "Oh, did that hurt you?" You say, "No, I don't care! It doesn't bother me at all!"

There are some powerful Scriptures that deal with pretense. Psalm 51:6 says, *Behold, You desire truth in the inner being; make me therefore to know wisdom in my inmost heart.*

I'm not going to live with bitterness — I'm going to have joy! I was a person with bitterness for too many years in my life. Inside, I was saying, "Who needs you? I'll make it on my own!" Well, I don't live like that anymore because I have received God's healing in my life.

Pretenders are unable to love and find it difficult to develop good relationships. Pretense is not limited to women. Many men pretend because of the macho attitude they think they should have. Sometimes men are hurting but won't admit it. They won't even let their own wives share the hurt. I think that makes women feel rejected because they want to share the hurts and the hard times as well as the good times.

John 8:32 says, *And you will know the Truth, and the Truth will set you free.* In fact, nothing but the Truth will set you free! Yet many of us who have tried to walk in faith have gotten mixed up about how to be honest with ourselves and with God...and also about how to walk in faith.

If you are sneezing every two seconds, water is running out of your eyes and somebody says, "Oh, you're sick," you don't have to say, "No, I'm not sick." You say, "But if I admit I'm sick, how will I get healed? I'm believing for healing!" Why not say this: "I'm not feeling well — you discerned that right. My body has a lot of symptoms right now, but I'm believing God for healing. Even though I'm not feeling great right now, I believe that *...greater is he that is in* [me] *than he that is in the world* (1 John 4:4, KJV). So I'd appreciate it if you'd just join your faith with mine and believe that God is going to raise me up and lift me out of this thing." That's how you walk in faith. You don't have to lie and make other people think you're goofy.

What if a co-worker sees that you are obviously sick, but you say, "Oh, no, I'm not sick"? Later they notice the Christian bumper sticker on the back of your car; and they say, "Oh, one of THEM — one of those holier-than-thou people you can't talk to because they won't be real with you!"

Or how about when someone has hurt you; and they come to you later and say, "I'm sorry that I hurt you." Instead of saying, "Thank you," you say, "Oh, no problem. You didn't hurt me."

Why can't we learn to be real and truthful? One thing in my favor is that I'm honest. I was not always honest, but it's a gift from God! I don't believe I could have come through all the junk I had to endure if God had not gifted me with the ability to be honest.

People tell me all the time, "I really enjoy your teaching because you're so honest! You just tell it the way it is. And you don't act like you have never had any problems!" That is because I don't know any other way to be. I don't think I could teach if I had to play pretend games.

Dave and I try to be real with each other. Sometimes I'll tell him, "Dave, this happened to me, or that happened to me, and it just really hurt me. Pray for me that I will get over it and be okay."

For many years of my life, however, I was nothing but a big pretender — my whole life was pretense. There are many people who have major wounds and hurts, yet they pretend and say, "That doesn't bother me!" They are building up walls by pretending.

One of my associates, who studied psychology for a while, recently discussed defense mechanisms with me. He said that some people try to handle the death of a loved one by refusing to face it. They say to themselves, "No, that didn't happen. I won't face that!" But that's pretending. And you can't pretend — you must face reality! You have to say, "That person is gone, and it hurts! I'm going to miss that person because he or she was a major part of my life. But God is not finished with my life. He left me here, and there is still something here for me. So I am going to press through and find out what it is. I know I'm going to need a time of healing and restoration; but in Jesus, I'm going to make it!"

If you don't face reality when a loved one dies or during a loss of any kind — if you build up walls right away when you begin to feel the pain — you could end up hurting forever.

Have you ever been a pretender? Do you sometimes find it hard to be real with people?

Ephesians 4:15 tells us to ...*let our lives lovingly express truth [in all things, speaking truly, dealing truly, living truly]....* Now, speaking truth doesn't mean we should look at somebody and say, "Your hair really looks bad!" If we do that, we won't have many friends! I used to do a lot of that, too. I knew how to speak the truth, but I didn't have any wisdom. Ephesians 4:15 goes on to say, *Enfolded in love, let us grow up in every way and in all things into Him Who is the Head, [even] Christ.*

No, we don't have to go around pretending. We don't have to try to be tough or try to be super Christians! Rejection hurts! But we can survive it, without pretense, in Christ!

Rejection Protection Pattern #3: Self-Defense

We defend ourselves from rejection in different ways. Sometimes we defend ourselves with anger: "You're hurting me, so I'm going to get mad! I'll deflect the pain by getting mad at you. I'll make you more miserable than you're making me. You're hurting me, but I'll get you back!"

When someone hurts me, I want to sit that individual down and correct him and teach him how to live so he won't hurt me. See, I'm a good teacher, and this gift of teaching doesn't just function in the pulpit! But people aren't always receptive to being taught. So I have had to learn when to function in my gift and when to realize that I am not to try to teach everyone all the time.

When we tell people all the things they must do to make us happy, those things become laws to them. Here is an example of what I mean:

Dave is so good to me. He's just wonderful! But there are certain things he is better at than others. Dave has never been much of a gift buyer. Now, he'll buy me anything I want at any holiday — that is, anything we can afford. He'll say, "What do you want? Come on, I'll take you out and get it for you." But he always says, "What's the sense of my going out and buying it and then bringing it home? You always want to take it back anyway! You don't like the color, or this or that, or something else!"

But women don't care about whether or not they have to take a gift back. They just want to know that their husbands are out there, tromping all over the mall, trying to find it. Wives don't care whether they like their gifts or not — none of that makes any difference. They just want to know that their husbands went to the trouble of going out there. They want to know that it cost their husband something besides money.

Dave and I were out of town one Mother's Day weekend. My children had taken me out before we left on the trip, and we only had one of our daughters with us. It was just the three of us. I don't think anybody except me remembered that it was Mother's Day. Finally I said to my daughter, "Tell me Happy Mother's Day!" And she said, "Oh, Happy Mother's Day!"

Now, we were all going out to church and doing some running around, so we were busy. I said to Dave, "What did you get me for Mother's Day?" He said, "You can have whatever you want!" But I said, "No — what did **you get me** for Mother's Day?" "Well, what do you want?" he asked.

I fought off the temptation all day long to sit Dave down and say, "Now, honey, I would like to lovingly explain to you how this hurts me!" But that wouldn't have done any good! Do you know what would happen if I did that? The next holiday that came around, he would feel **obligated** to go out and buy something for me just to keep me happy. And it wouldn't mean anything to me if it didn't come from his heart.

We had some time that afternoon and I said, "Let's go to the mall!" When we got there, I asked, "Are you going to buy me a Mother's Day present?" And Dave said, "Sure. What do you want?" He bought me a beautiful outfit.

I might have liked it better if it had happened in a little different way, but the whole point is that Dave loves me and has so many great qualities and does a lot of things that other people don't do, so why should I care about that one thing?

No matter who you are around, people are not going to do things to please you 100 percent. So I resist the temptation to sit Dave, or anyone else down, and tell them how they should treat me so I won't be hurt. **We should turn our defense over to the Lord.**

When we try to lay out a lot of guidelines for our relationships, it's a sneaky method of self-defense! We are trying to tell people how to treat us so we won't have to build up walls to protect ourselves! When we try to impart such revelation to someone else, we end up with what amounts to legalism! But if we let God impart that revelation to them, they'll learn something; and it will be done permanently...with joy.

Rejection Protection Pattern #4: Verbal Defense

When we use the protection pattern of verbal defense, we try to convince others that we're right.

It is interesting to note that Jesus never defended Himself. The Bible says that He entrusted Himself to God in everything. In the midst of being abused, He entrusted everything, including Himself, to the One Who judges fairly (see 1 Peter 2:23). Jesus went about doing God's business — doing good and, in particular, curing all who were oppressed of the devil.

When we entrust ourselves totally to God and get busy doing His work instead of spending all of our time trying to protect ourselves, our self-constructed walls will come down. We need to let our lives convince others that our hearts are in the right place instead of trying to convince them by defending ourselves verbally.

If you have taken up your own defense, I ask you to remember that Jesus is your Advocate. That means He is your lawyer — the One Who will plead your case. Let Him be your defense.

Rejection Protection Pattern #5: Buying Protection

Do you bless other people because you love them, or do you do it to get them to love you? There was a time in my life when I tried to buy protection so that no one would reject me. I thought if I was extremely nice to people and gave them gifts, I could protect myself from their rejection. In certain relationships, when I wanted to make sure I was accepted and not rejected, I really turned it on.

But I was deceived in that. I really thought I was walking in love until God revealed to me that I was not giving my love freely to others without strings attached. I was giving to others in order to get them to love me — to keep them from rejecting me.

When you give a gift, it should always be for the joy of giving, not with the ulterior motive of trying to manipulate the recipient in some way so that they feel they owe you something.

Sometimes many of us think, "Well, I'll keep you from ever rejecting me! I'll just treat you so wonderfully...I'll be so good to you...I'll do so many great things for you that you will just want to be around me all the time!"

One lady I know has a tremendous root of rejection in her life — a terrible spirit of insecurity — and she ruins relationships by suffocating people. The minute she finds somebody who will pay any attention to her and with whom she might develop a relationship — whether it is a lady friend or somebody she would like to date — she starts sending presents and cards and calling them on the phone too often. She just goes overboard. Her behavior is way out of balance.

If you asked this lady, she would tell you that she was being led by the Spirit. She would say, "Well, I'm just trying to be nice to people!" But she is not facing the reality that she tries to buy friendship. She tries to buy herself protection from rejection!

When things get out of balance in our lives, we can become overbearing. Then our well-intentioned actions have an opposite effect than we intended on other people. Why? Because people can sense when something is not being done with the right spirit.

What are the rejection protection patterns in your life? You need to identify them so God can minister freedom to you — freedom from the root of rejection!

6

Rejection and Perfection

In dealing with people, you must remember that it is impossible for them to behave perfectly. It is impossible for people, no matter how wonderful they are, to never make mistakes or say the wrong thing at the wrong time. Yet one of the things that causes problems in relationships is the **unrealistic** expectation of perfection.

We humans have a tendency to try to change others. We want to train them in such a way that they will never hurt us. We seek to live in an "incubator-type lifestyle," where nothing can ever get to us or shake us.

Many people spend a large part of their lives declaring, "I'm not going to get hurt!" They go to extremes to protect themselves from rejection. They live lives of horrible loneliness because they withdraw and refuse to get involved with people. Other people get involved to a certain point; but when a relationship begins to become intimate, they back off and refuse any further involvement.

In protecting themselves from one type of pain, these individuals create another type of suffering. Loneliness is painful! It is painful to watch other people interacting with each other and having good relationships while you remain all alone. If you are one of these individuals, I believe this book will help you. I believe there is a unique anointing on this teaching to bring freedom to those who have been suffering from the pain of rejection!

Perfection: A Means of Protection

In the last chapter, we discussed various ways a rejected person attempts to protect himself from further emotional pain. We learned that one of those rejection protection patterns is buying protection. In this chapter, we'll learn how people try to buy rejection protection through their own perfectionism.

What is perfectionism? It's saying, "I'm going to keep you from ever rejecting me! I'll be perfect, and then you will never be able to find anything wrong with me! And if you can't find anything wrong with me, you will just naturally love me! You'll never reject me because I'll never do anything to get you upset or rattle you!"

The dictionary defines *perfection* as lacking nothing essential; being of the highest excellence, flawless, exact, faultless, without defect, and being supremely excellent. The definition is correct from a worldly standpoint but not as far as a person's spiritual life is concerned. When you look up *perfection* in the Bible, a Greek dictionary or even in *The Amplified Bible*, it has an entirely different connotation.

The biblical definition of *perfection* is to grow to complete maturity.[1] It does not mean that right now, right this minute, you must not be doing anything wrong! What the word actually means in the biblical sense is that we are to be people who are pressing toward the mark of perfection.

Are you trying to be perfect through hard work? Are you a workaholic? Are you suffering under the burden of never feeling okay...never feeling that you are good enough...always feeling just a little unacceptable? Do you

---

[1]Based on the following:

James Strong, "Greek Dictionary of the New Testament," Strong's Exhaustive Concordance of the Bible (Nashville: Abingdon, 1890), p. 71, #5052.

Vine, Vol. III, pp. 175, 176.

feel if you could just do better and make less mistakes, then maybe God would love you more and answer your prayers more often...and then maybe people would accept you? That's a lie!

Most people with the root of rejection suffer unbearably with the problem of perfectionism. I suffered with it during much of my life. God has done a great work in my life in this area, but I find that He is constantly bringing me into more freedom from perfectionism.

God wants us to be happy. Jesus said, ...*I came that they may have and enjoy life, and have it in abundance (to the full, till it overflows)* (John 10:10). He wants us to enjoy life!

I've discovered that if I can only enjoy life on the days when I've done everything right, there won't be many days when I can lean back and say, "I can really enjoy this day!" No, we don't have to buy our joy with perfection!

Two Paths to Perfection

God has shown me that there are two paths to perfection — the legal way and the illegal way. The legal way to perfection is to be made perfect through the blood of the Lamb, Jesus Christ. He is the only Perfect One. We are to identify with Him as we *press toward the mark for the prize of the high calling of God...* (Philippians 3:14, KJV).

This thing called perfection has some interesting aspects. On one hand, the Bible commands us to be perfect. Then it says we cannot be perfect in our own works. That always frustrated me! I would say, "Lord, why are You telling me to do something on one page, and telling me on another page that I cannot do it?" I had not yet come to understand that Jesus, the perfect One, is seated at the right hand of the Father, constantly making intercession for me. And through His intercession, every one of my imperfections is made perfect. I get the benefit of His perfection through faith!

I didn't understand that truth — so I worked and worked...struggled and struggled...tried and tried...because I loved God and wanted to be good and do everything right! And I kept failing...and failing...and failing! I got mad at myself! I hated myself! And I tried harder and harder! That's one supposed path to perfection...but it's the wrong path! It does not work.

God finally told me, "People on that plan are on a plan of their own works, efforts and struggles. Those people are trying to buy perfection with their works! They are trying to get it illegally!" That's when He revealed to me that there is only one legal way to be made perfect, and that is through believing in Jesus, the perfect One! We know that, even though we don't see perfection right now in every area of our lives, we see Jesus! I like that! The Bible says all things are under our feet; and we have authority over all things, even though we don't yet see all things under our feet. Nevertheless, we see Jesus!

I believe by faith that I am in the process of manifesting completion or perfection. My heart's desire is to be perfect. Therefore, I believe God counts me as perfect while I am making the trip. I believe I am perfect (complete) "in Christ." I didn't understand for a long time. I thought, "Well, if I am so perfect, why do I keep doing things I don't want to do? Why do I keep making mistakes and doing things that are wrong?"

Please Consider These Scriptures:

First Thessalonians 5:22-24 says: *Abstain from evil [shrink from it and keep aloof from it] in whatever form or whatever kind it may be. And may the God of peace Himself sanctify you through and through [separate you from profane things, make you pure and wholly consecrated to God]; and may your spirit and soul and body be preserved sound and complete [and found] blameless at the coming of our Lord Jesus Christ (The Messiah). Faithful is He who is calling you [to Himself] and utterly trustworthy, and He will also do it [fulfill His call by hallowing and keeping you].*

Hebrews 13:20,21 says: *Now may the God of peace [Who is the Author and the Giver of peace], Who brought again from among the dead our Lord Jesus, that great Shepherd of the sheep, by the blood [that sealed, ratified] the everlasting agreement (covenant, testament), Strengthen (complete, perfect) and make you what you ought to be and equip you with everything good that you may carry out His will; [while He Himself] works in you and accomplishes that which is pleasing in His sight, through Jesus Christ (the Messiah); to Whom be the glory forever and ever (to the ages of the ages). Amen.*

First Peter 5:10 says: *And after you have suffered a little while, the God of all grace [Who imparts all blessing and favor], Who has called you to His [own] eternal glory in Christ Jesus, will Himself complete and make you what you ought to be, establish and ground you securely, and strengthen, and settle you.*

Press Toward the Mark

Remember what I said earlier, "If you have a perfect heart toward God and you are pressing toward the mark of perfection, He counts you as perfect while you're making the trip." He sees your heart. The Bible says, *For the eyes of the Lord run to and fro throughout the whole earth, to shew himself strong in the behalf of them whose heart is perfect toward him...* (2 Chronicles 16:9, KJV). I used to read and hear only the first part of that verse: "The eyes of God roam to and fro across the face of the earth...looking for someone" — and I would get scared! I would think, "Oh, my! God is looking! I need to shape up because He needs me! The world is in a mess! How can God use me in the condition I'm in?"

Then one day, by His grace and mercy, God caused me to read this entire verse: *For the eyes of the Lord run to and fro throughout the whole earth to show Himself strong in behalf of those whose hearts are blameless toward Him.*

Philippians 1:6 says, *And I am convinced and sure of this very thing, that He Who began a good work in you will continue* — not just for three weeks...or a year...and then it will be done — but *until the day of Jesus Christ [right up to the time of His return].*

You're making progress as you keep pressing toward the mark of perfection! God showed me something powerful about this process. He said, **"Every single person is at a different place on the road of life!"** Think about it! We all got saved at different times. We have different backgrounds, and some of us have deeper hurts than others. Some people press a little harder than others. Thank God, He has a personalized plan for our lives!

The Lord showed me that, when the trumpet sounds and Jesus comes, Christians will be in many varied places along the road of life. We're not all in the same place now in our outward manifestation of the perfection in Christ, and we won't all be at the same place then. But if each of us has a perfect heart toward God, He sees each one of us as equal. Those who are not quite as perfected as others simply need Jesus a little more. But He's got enough perfection to go around!

We serve the Perfect One, and He is interceding for us right now. Jesus is sitting at the right hand of the Father, praying for me as I write this book, so that every imperfect thing I do will be made to work out perfectly.

I used to work hard at trying to do everything just right so people wouldn't reject me. I would think, "What if I say or do the wrong things and people don't like it?" That was hard work! I was trying to buy perfection illegally! I wasn't looking to Jesus — the Perfect One.

One day God said, "Joyce, you don't need to worry about how far you have progressed when the trumpet blows! Wherever you are on the road of life, you'll be all right!" I don't know whether I'll be halfway finished, a quarter of the way finished or three-quarters finished, but Jesus knows!

Look at the Scriptures below. Please pay careful attention to how many times the words *perfect* and *perfecting* appear in these passages.

*And I am convinced and sure of this very thing, that He Who began a good work in you will continue until the day of Jesus Christ [right up to the time of His return], developing [that good work] and **perfecting** and bringing it to full completion in you* (Philippians 1:6).

*Not that I have now attained [this ideal], or have already been made **perfect**, but I press on to lay hold of (grasp) and make my own, that for which Christ Jesus (the Messiah) has laid hold of me and made me His own. I do not consider, brethren, that I have captured and made it my own [yet]; but one thing I do [it is my one aspiration]: forgetting what lies behind and straining forward to what lies ahead, I press on toward the goal...* (Philippians 3:12-14).

In this passage, the Apostle Paul — who received as much as three-fourths of the New Testament from God by revelation — is admitting that he has not yet been made perfect! I don't know about you, but that takes the pressure off me for Paul to say, "I don't even consider that I'm perfected yet!" In light of that, I don't have to get up every day **trying** to be perfect! I just need to get up every day, **determined** to press on...forgetting what lies behind and straining forward to what lies ahead. That means the mistakes of twenty-five years ago (and the mistakes I made five minutes ago) must be left behind!

Make a Decision

If you are like me, you will have to make a decision to press on many times each day. When I say things to my husband that I wish I hadn't said, even though I'm trying so hard to be a submissive wife, I have to press on! I think to myself, "There I go again — I did it! I talked back! And I was believing God to help me keep my mouth shut!" Then I say, "God, will I never be able to keep my mouth shut?" Do you know what His answer is? "Repent...let it go...and press on!"

If you don't press on, you will always be trapped in your past mistakes. If you want to make progress, you'll move forward a lot faster if you don't waste time worrying about all the things you didn't do right.

Paul spoke of pressing toward the goal. What is the goal? Perfection! To be like Jesus is the goal of Christians! That is my goal! I want to be Christ-like! I want to be like Jesus and respond like Jesus in every situation!

Sometimes, when I argue with Dave, I get aggravated at myself. I've gotten better about it, thank God! Sometimes Dave tells me, "You are like a different woman than the woman you were years ago! You have changed so much!" But I still don't always do everything perfectly.

One day I was having a particularly rough day, and it seemed that I repeatedly challenged Dave and tried to get my own way. By the end of the day, I thought, "What's the deal? Am I ever going to get to the point where I can shut my mouth?"

Then the Lord said to me, "Joyce, you are getting better all the time. Do you know what makes Me happy? That you care. So many people act like that day and night and couldn't care less what I think about their behavior! I am blessed when My people care about what I think — when they don't want to act badly, and they grieve over their sins and inabilities."

And all of a sudden, the pressure that had been building up inside me just vanished! Whoever would have thought about being just a little bit happy with themselves for caring what God thinks about them? Instead, we feel a load of pressure as we try to buy perfection through our works. And the price is high — it costs us our joy!

7

Perfect...by Faith!

The pressure to be perfect will steal your joy! You won't have any time for joy. You won't have any time to just rest in God and enjoy life. You won't even have time to enjoy God. For many years, I was so busy trying to serve God perfectly that I didn't have time to enjoy Him. When this happens, Christianity becomes a labor.

Sometimes we use our "faith" to believe God for houses, cars, prosperity, mates, children, businesses, healings or success; and we forget to believe Him to perfect us! We take on that job ourselves! Every day, we get up with a list of things that we're not going to do...and we forget to get God involved, so we fail.

While Jesus is interceding for us at the Father's right hand, He must be saying, "They still don't have the message! They still don't understand that, apart from Me, they can do nothing!"

There is only one way to get perfection legally, and that's through faith in the blood of Jesus Christ. You can't get it any other way.

Tell me, you who are bent on being under the Law, will you listen to what the Law [really] says? (Galatians 4:21). The Old Testament law said, "If you do **all** of this, you'll be okay!" But it was impossible to keep **all** of those laws. It was labor...it was hard work! It stole the joy of the people. Let me paraphrase Galatians 4:21: "Tell me, you who are bent on trying to buy perfection with your works...will you listen to what the Law really says?"

Then in the remainder of Galatians 4, the Holy Spirit proceeds to contrast the Old Covenant with the New Covenant. One was a covenant of works, of trying to achieve perfection ourselves. The other was the covenant of promise, where God says, "All I am asking you to do is believe Me! Keep your eyes on Me, and I will bring these things to pass in due time!" One is a covenant of works and the other is of faith. And so it is in every area of our lives. Galatians 3:10 says that those who live under the Law are *doomed to disappointment.*

However, many people never think to apply faith in the area of achieving perfection. One of my most popular messages is on God's grace. I call it "Grace, Grace and More Grace — Plus!" When God gave me that message, I was about to kill myself with works. I was busy night and day, trying to buy perfection with my own effort; and I was paying a high price. I was giving up my joy. I was giving up my health. I was burned out...my mind was a mess. I was miserable.

That kind of labor actually steals a person's strength. It just wears you out and makes you tired. Jesus said in Matthew 11:28, *Come to Me, all you who labor and are heavy-laden and overburdened, and I will cause you to rest. [I will ease and relieve and refresh your souls.]* Many Christians drag themselves around in the works of their own flesh trying to serve God. They spend so much time trying to be good that they don't even have the energy to pray, let alone really enjoy God or the "Kingdom living" He offers.

If there was any hope of my living a perfect life on my own, I don't believe Jesus would have taken the job of being my continual Intercessor when He left His earthly ministry. Why do we need an Intercessor? Because there is a breach between us and God, and we don't know how to bridge the gap. So God put an Intercessor there to stand in the gap and make up the difference.

As long as I am in this earthly body, there will always be a gap between me and God. God is perfect in all His ways, and I am not! But Jesus, my Intercessor, is filling that gap — He is perfect! He is standing in the gap for me day and night. When I leave this earth and go to heaven, He won't need to do that anymore. But while I am here, He is my perfection. I am complete in Christ.

God Chooses Us...On Purpose

The Bible says that God purposely chooses the weak and foolish things of the world in order that He might use those weak, foolish things to confound the wise (see 1 Corinthians 1:27, KJV). He wants those who are wise in themselves to look at those of us who are being used by God and say, "...You?" **He wants to astound them!**

Several years ago, just after God called me into the ministry, He gave me a vision about how He planned to use me. I was immature so I was telling people about it! A young girl approached me one night at a church party and said, "Somebody told me you said that you think you're going to have one of the biggest ministries run by a woman in this whole nation! Did you really say that?"

I said, "Yes, I believe that's what God told me." She said, "Frankly, with your personality, I don't see how that could ever happen!" She actually said that to me!

In the beginning, I had enough fleshly pride to think, "Well!" But God had to humble me to the point that I knew it could not happen either, without God. I had to face myself as I was and begin to say, "I can do nothing without You, Lord."

God wants to put us in positions where the world will look at us and say, "That has to be the power of God in operation!"

Why do you think Jesus chose the disciples He chose? If He had been looking for perfection, He probably wouldn't have picked tax collectors and fishermen! Tax collectors were hated in Jesus' day — they were the worst of the worst. Nobody could stand tax collectors! Yet Jesus said to Matthew, "I can use you! Follow Me!" All he had to do to qualify was to follow Him. Jesus didn't give the prospective disciples an application and say, "Tell Me all your qualifications!" He didn't say, "Well, you can hang out with Me for a couple of weeks, and I'll watch and see how many mistakes you make." All He said was, "Follow Me! Be My disciples! Learn about Me and desire to be like Me, and I will make you fishers of men! I'll use you!"

Yes, God chooses the weak and foolish things of this world, on purpose, so that people will look at them and say, "It has to be God!" That's what He wants! He wants to use us and have people know it's Him.

I tell people all over the country, "You wouldn't believe the mess I was in, and the wreck I was. You wouldn't believe the past I had. And look what God is doing now!" What can you say, except, "That has to be God!" But if He had started out with somebody who had no problems — somebody who was all polished and could say everything just right — people might have given the credit to Joyce Meyer instead of to God. God and I don't have any problem with Who gets the credit — I know where my ability is coming from! And the days when I make mistakes serve as painful reminders!

I read this statement recently: "God leaves glaring imperfections in some of His choicest saints, on purpose, just to keep them in a position where He can use them." Think about that! How proud and haughty do you think we would be if we could get through even three days without making one mistake? What do you think we would be like? Why, immediately we would become everybody's teacher. Every imperfect person in the world would now have to sit under our perfect instruction and let us tell them how to become perfect — like us! We would be proud and haughty, and it would prevent God from using us. God uses humble men and women, not those who think they are capable in themselves.

Striving for Christian Maturity

Christian maturity is not necessarily doing everything perfectly or never making a mistake. It is knowing Christ and the power of HIS resurrection. We know that we will make mistakes, but if we admit our sins and sincerely repent, He is faithful to forgive us and cleanse us from all unrighteousness. (1 John 1:9.) I believe a mature Christian has learned how to stay under The Blood instead of under condemnation.

In Philippians 3, Paul said that he had not arrived at the ideal place of perfection, but he was determined to press on toward the mark. In a portion of verse 15, he continues: *So let those [of us] who are spiritually mature and full-grown have this mind and hold these convictions....* A mature Christian is certainly going to try to do his very best every day and do it for the right reason, which is his love for Jesus. We are made right with God through the sacrifice and bloodshed of Jesus Christ, not through our effort to please God. Don't spend your life trying to please God so that He will love you or bless you more. God is love. He loves you unconditionally before you ever pay any attention to Him at all. He promised to never reject you if you **believe** in Him.

A mature Christian knows that, even at his very best, he will still make mistakes. He also knows that to live under condemnation, self-hatred and self-rejection will not help him live a holier life. THE MATURE CHRISTIAN DOES HIS BEST AND TRUSTS JESUS TO DO THE REST.

The devil is always there to condemn you when you make even the smallest mistake. He wants you to spend your days feeling bad about yourself — feeling like a failure. Don't fall into the devil's trap. When you're under condemnation, it is hard to pray or to serve God in any capacity. Guilt and condemnation leave you under tremendous pressure, and there are many other negative side effects. They can do everything from making you difficult to get along with to bringing on physical sickness. Another thing that happens is that we put a burden on others to be perfect if we live under that burden ourselves. Unrealistic expectations place great strain on relationships. It ruins many marriages as well as all other kinds of relationships, including those between parents and their children. In other words, perfectionists will demand perfection from others as well as themselves.

Children need correction but not rejection. They need acceptance and unconditional love. We need to be able to show mercy to others and not be legalistic, rigid and hard to please. Giving mercy requires receiving mercy! Remember, if you are excessively hard on yourself, it may cause you to be the same way with other people. Jesus said in Matthew 11:29,30: *Take My yoke upon you and learn of Me, for I am gentle (meek) and humble (lowly) in heart, and you will find rest (relief and ease and refreshment and recreation and blessed quiet) for your souls. For My yoke is wholesome (useful, good — not harsh, hard, sharp, or pressing, but comfortable, gracious, and pleasant), and My burden is light and easy to be borne.*

We should never try to put a burden on ourselves or anyone else that Jesus would not place there. The Spirit of Jesus is patient, longsuffering, forbearing and slow to anger. We have His Spirit in us and can learn to behave the way He would in relationships.

Do you want to find out if you are a mature Christian? Living under condemnation is not a sign of maturity. Maturity demands that your attitude be: "I'm pressing toward the mark of perfection. I haven't arrived yet — I haven't attained; but I am going to keep pressing toward that goal. I have made a decision that I am not going to live under guilt and condemnation. I am not going to live my life constantly trying to figure out what is wrong with me. One thing I'm going to do: I'm going to forget what lies behind (my mistakes) and press on to what lies ahead (greater victory over the flesh every day)."

Remember, condemnation is a feeling that the devil produces when we make mistakes, and we receive the feeling as truth if we do not know that our value and worth are in Christ and not in our works. We live by faith and not by feelings.

What is perfection in God's eyes? It is a perfect heart toward God — someone who wants to do everything right and is pressing toward that mark. It is a person who loves Jesus with his whole heart. I read an interesting article recently that said many people love Jesus, but they are not "in love" with Him. How do you act when you are in love with someone? You have him on your mind all the time, and you chase after him, always wanting to be with him and do things for him. That's how we should be about Jesus! We need to fall in love with Him because He died for us on the cross. We should chase after Him like a deer pants and longs for the water brooks. Psalm 42:1 says, *As the hart (deer) pants and longs for the water brooks, so I pant and long for You, O God.*

God is looking for people with perfect hearts, not a perfect performance. We get a lot more concerned about our weaknesses than He does. He knows that our weaknesses are simply places where He might show Himself strong in us.

We reject ourselves and others because of imperfection. Other people reject us because of imperfection. GOD NEVER REJECTS US BECAUSE OF OUR IMPERFECTIONS OR WEAKNESSES. DEPEND ON GOD!

Paul had taught the Galatians about their liberty in Christ — that their worth was "in Christ" and not in their own works. They apparently had gained some revelation on this truth and were beginning to walk in it and enjoy it. However, the devil was not going to leave them alone, and he will not leave you alone either. He will try on a regular basis to bring you back under the Law — the Law of perfection by following all the rules and regulations and never making a mistake. Paul instructed them not only to strive to be free but also to stand fast in their liberty and freedom.

They had gained a certain measure of freedom, and then Paul saw that they were changing again and going back to where they had come from. They were giving up their liberty and going back under bondage to the Law. He said in Galatians 3:1, *O you poor and silly and thoughtless... Galatians! Who has fascinated or bewitched or cast a spell over you...?* Yes, Satan will try to prevent you from ever getting free from the fear of rejection and the fear of imperfection. And whatever freedom you do gain, he will try to steal again. That is one reason why I keep saying the same things over and over in this book in several different ways.

I know it takes a lot of revelation to bring complete deliverance to those who are in the "performance-acceptance trap." Bringing freedom to those who have lived their lives trying to avoid rejection through perfection is one of my greatest joys. I suffered so much in this area myself that I delight in being able to help others see the truth.

Galatians 3:2,3 says: *Let me ask you this one question: Did you receive the [Holy] Spirit as the result of obeying the Law and doing its works, or was it by hearing [the message of the Gospel] and believing [it]? [Was it from observing a law of rituals or from a message of faith?] Are you so foolish and so senseless and so silly? Having begun [your new life spiritually] with the [Holy] Spirit, are you now reaching perfection [by dependence] on the flesh?*

Paul had taught these Christians that they no longer had to live under the Law because they were now living in the dispensation of grace, and so are we. The dispensation of grace is a time period in which people do not have to live under the Law to gain perfection. God will write His law in their hearts and on their minds, and He will put His Spirit within them. Their perfection will be found only in Christ and by placing all confidence in Him and putting all dependence upon Him. The time they had read about under the Old Covenant had arrived, but they were having a hard time believing it and sticking with it. Why? I think the message of the Gospel is so simple that we look for something harder; and it is, like the old saying goes, almost too good to be true. Therefore, our minds have a hard time taking it in and being convinced.

You need plenty of continued revelation in this area, especially if you are a person who has come from a background of rejection and low self-esteem. As you CONTINUE in God's Word, you will keep gaining more and more freedom in these areas and learn how to keep the freedom you gain.

We rarely ever go from bondage to complete freedom overnight. It happens in degrees. Second Corinthians 3:18 calls it *degrees of glory*. We are changed from glory to glory. Do not be discouraged if your progress seems to be slow. **Slow progress is better than no progress,** and you're probably not moving any slower than most people. Keep going back to God as often as you need to and asking for more revelation and more freedom in these areas. Remember, He never gets tired of seeing you before His throne asking for help.

I can't tell you how many times I went through this in my life! God gave me revelation along these lines, and I would move up higher. For a long period of time, the devil could not hang guilt and condemnation on me. Then I would seem to slip back into old ways, and I would need to study and seek God again in this area. I did it over and over and over. Actually, it took years of fresh revelation in this area to get me to the place of freedom I now enjoy.

Once again, please do not be discouraged if you need to go over and over the same ground. The Holy Spirit is patient, and He will work with you however long it takes to see you have complete freedom. Depend on Him entirely to reveal to you what you need to see. Don't think that God's expectations are like man's. He knows that we all have inbred weaknesses. About three years ago, God gave me wonderful revelation about weaknesses...and how every single human being has them. He revealed to me that as long as I was in a fleshly body, I would make some mistakes!

Everybody makes mistakes! Once I finally understood that, I was delivered from pressuring myself (and others) to be perfect.

The Bible repeatedly says, "Grace and peace be multiplied to you." Notice that grace comes before peace. I had to know how to receive God's grace before I could have peace. Grace is God's enablement coming to me to help me do what I could not do without Him. God leaves us in a position where WE MUST DEPEND ON HIM AND HIM ALONE. First Corinthians 13:10 says, *But when the complete and perfect...comes, the incomplete and imperfect will vanish away....*

When Jesus comes back to get us, all that is fragmentary and imperfect will be done away with. Until then, I get the privilege of depending on Him, and so do you. What does all this have to do with rejection? Everything! People try to pay the price of perfection so others won't reject them. People try hard to be perfect so that God won't reject them — even though He has reassured us many times in His Word that He loves us and will never reject us. It is the **feelings** that get to us sometimes. We feel! We feel! We feel!

We **feel** that we must buy God's acceptance. The price? Our own perfection!

Are you receiving understanding of how rejection and perfection are relatives? Remember, Jesus said, *...I came that they may have and enjoy life, and have it in abundance (to the full, till it overflows)* (John 10:10).

As you are reading this book, I believe you are having your eyes opened; and you will stop trying to buy protection from rejection through perfection! I believe you are facing a new day in your life of being able to enjoy God, yourself and life more than ever before. Depend on Him; do not depend on the Law.

Let me quote Galatians 3:10 again: *And all who depend on the Law [who are seeking to be justified by obedience to the Law of rituals] are under a curse and doomed to disappointment....* I don't want you to have to live like that anymore. God does not want you to have to live under that burden anymore, and I am sure you don't want to live that way anymore. Working...working...working...and always being disappointed because, although you tried so hard, you did not achieve the desired result. Self-improvement does not come through self-effort; it comes from dependence upon God — from faith in Him.

He allows us to make an effort, but it must be effort made while depending on Him, not effort apart from Him. Let's read again our ever-popular Scripture, John 15:5: *I am the Vine; you are the branches. Whoever lives in Me and I in him bears much (abundant) fruit. However, apart from Me [cut off from vital union with Me] you can do nothing.* No, we don't have to live under the curse of disappointment. Each time you fail and feel disappointed in yourself, look to Jesus — the Perfect One!

What about rejection from others? Jesus said, "Don't worry about it. If they are rejecting you, they are rejecting Me!" That's what He told the seventy disciples when He sent them out. Obviously, they had been concerned about whether or not they would be rejected. Jesus said, "If they reject you, they reject Me!" Keep your eyes on Jesus! He was rejected, too! But the Bible says, ...*The very Stone which the builders rejected and threw away has become the Cornerstone...* (Matthew 21:42). If you keep your eyes on Jesus, those who reject you will one day look on, as God Himself raises you up and causes you to be like the chief Cornerstone — right before their very eyes! Those who rejected you will look at you and say, "I can't believe it!" And you will say, "I can't either!" But the Bible says, ...*With men this is impossible, but all things are possible with God!* (Matthew 19:26).

I used to worry about what a mess I was until the day I received a revelation that God made everything we see out of nothing. I thought, "Well, God, if You made everything we see out of nothing, surely You could do a little bit more with a mess! So I'll just give You this mess that I am!" I mean, if He made the trees and the sun and the moon and the stars and the sky and the mountains and the ocean out of nothing, just think what He could do with a mess! I don't know about you, but that gave me hope!

Hebrews 7:25 says, *Therefore He is able also to save to the uttermost (completely, perfectly, finally, and for all time and eternity) those who come to God through Him, since He is always living to make petition to God and intercede with Him and intervene for them.* Wow! What a Scripture! He is able to save me to the uttermost — that means through and through. Jesus is able to save me from whatever is wrong with me! I can't save myself and neither can you! But Jesus can save me, and He can save you!

God has done something in my life that has brought me freedom. When I make a mistake, I am now able to take it to the Lord right away. I don't mess around with feeling guilty about it for three hours. I just take it right to Him and say, "Jesus — You're the Perfect One. Your blood is still on that mercy seat in the heavenly Holy of Holies. Your blood is crying out, 'Mercy, mercy, mercy for Joyce Meyer!' Right now, Jesus, You are interceding for me before the Father! I depend on You."

As an example of what I mean by this, suppose I went to the theater and tried to get in with an imperfect ticket. The ticket-taker would say, "I can't let you in, lady. There's something wrong with your ticket! It's not perfect. The number is worn off, the corner has been chewed off and I can't let you in." But if I know the manager of that theater and he is standing nearby, he could step over to the ticket-taker to say, "She's a personal friend of mine. Let her in." That ticket-taker would have to change his decision and say, "No problem! Come right in!"

Well, I'm going to be bold and say, "I'm a personal friend of Jesus! He is my personal Friend! And if there is anything wrong with my ticket, He'll take care of it! I am depending on Him."

8

The Fear of Man

The fear of man causes us to be men-pleasers instead of God-pleasers. When a person has the root of rejection in him, he can easily fall into the trap of man-pleasing. We want to please people because that will keep them from rejecting us. Right?

This is such a deceptive and dangerous area. First of all, if that is the way you get your friends, that is the way you will have to keep or maintain those friendships. A lifetime of man-pleasing that is birthed out of the fear of man and the fear of rejection is terrible bondage.

In this chapter, I would like to help you realize that being a man-pleaser instead of a God-pleaser is sin! Perhaps you have never thought of it that way. Romans 14:23 (KJV) says, *...whatsoever is not of faith is sin.* When I was a man-pleaser, I certainly wasn't doing it by faith. I was operating in the FEAR of man, not FAITH in God.

What is sin? If you study the word *sin*, you will learn that its literal meaning is "to miss the mark"[1] — to fall short of God's will. It is God's will for us to follow the leading of the Holy Spirit, not the demands of people.

Now this certainly does not mean that we can never do anything someone else wants us to, but it does mean that God's will for us must always have first place. We must not

---

[1] Strong, "Greek Dictionary of the New Testament," p. 10, #2640.

do what people want us to just to keep them from getting upset with us or rejecting us if what they want is going to keep us out of the will of God. We should always choose to be God-pleasers and not men-pleasers.

I have spent a lot of time in this book trying to help you come out from under condemnation if that has been a problem in your life. I certainly don't intend to open a door now for the enemy. I know that, even as I write these lines, I am addressing some people who have fallen into the trap of being men-pleasers. When I say it is sin, I am trying to open your eyes to the seriousness of it. I am certainly not trying to put you under condemnation. We must learn the difference between conviction and condemnation. God often uses me to bring conviction. He uses His Word and His Spirit to bring us up higher.

I am writing this under the influence of the Holy Spirit, and He convicts people of sin, but He never condemns them. God brings conviction so that we can see our errors, admit them, be truly sorry, repent and receive the power of the Holy Spirit. We can then allow Him to enable us to walk free from that thing which has been sin in our lives.

According to Hebrews 4:15, Jesus understands our weaknesses and our infirmities. He certainly does! But He does not want people to use His understanding nature as an excuse to stay in sin that is producing bondage in their lives.

Breaking free of the fear of man and a man-pleasing spirit is not easy. It requires a revelation on exactly what it is and how devastating it can be. It requires serious determination to become free. Controlling and manipulating spirits are involved, and they do not give up their ground easily.

For years I excused myself and made little or no progress because I said to myself, "I just can't help it. I was abused, I just have these fears and I can't help it." These are some of the excuses that keep many people in bondage. The excuses may be completely factual, but the truth of God's Word has enough power to override facts.

Yes, Jesus understands, but He does not want you to stay in bondage to the fear of man. I believe God has you reading this book because He wants to set you free in this area or to help you recognize these spirits when they are attacking you. I believe your love for God, your desire to be in His will and your refusal to allow the enemy to run your life through manipulative and controlling spirits can help you attack the sin of man-pleasing in a bold manner.

God gives us free choice and free will. He wants us to choose Him and His ways, but He will not force us into it. Satan, on the other hand, has no problem using force, manipulation, control or anything else he can use to prevent us from being free. The devil uses the root of rejection that is in so many people. The fear of rejection and the fear of man are really the same thing. The fear of man — fear of losing approval, fear of being lonely, fear of being talked about or made fun of, fear of what people will say or think of us, and many other fears keep us from following the leading of the Holy Spirit. The devil knows that God has a good plan for your life, and his goal is to prevent you from ever having it.

If you want to be free from these spirits I am un-covering, you must be willing to confront them. You will never get free from them by running, avoiding or procrastinating. We must face issues and know that Jesus is always with us to strengthen and help us. The only way to get on the other side of a problem and eliminate its power over you is to face it and allow the Holy Spirit to instruct you on how to walk through it.

I will never gain a personal victory if I always get deliverance by miracles. God may give us some victories in that way, but all of them won't come that way. He wants to empower us to face the enemy ourselves (in the strength of His power) so that we can have a personal victory.

Fear Not!

We know that the Bible says, *Fear not...*, but for some reason, we have the idea that God is saying, "Don't **feel** fear!" There was a time in my life when I thought **feeling** fear indicated that I was a coward. When I felt fear, I felt bad about myself. Many times, when I was ready to go forward in some area, I would suddenly feel afraid. I prayed for the day when I would no longer be afraid! In fact, I went to other people and asked them to pray that I wouldn't be in fear anymore! But God gave me a life-changing revelation about fear a few years ago, and I occasionally have to remind myself of it.

Throughout the Bible, God says, *Fear not...fear not...fear not!* He is warning us about the spirit of fear. He is saying, "A spirit of fear can attack you and keep you from going forward."

It is recorded in the first chapter of Joshua that God told Joshua he would be finishing up the job God had given to Moses. Joshua 1:9 says, *...Be strong, vigorous, and very courageous. Be not afraid, neither be dismayed, for the Lord your God is with you wherever you go.*

If fear had not been about to attack Joshua, why would God have warned him? God was actually saying to Joshua, "I'm sending you to do a job. But, Joshua, just as sure as I'm talking to you, fear is going to be the enemy that will try to keep you from doing it!" Was God forbidding Joshua to **feel** fear? No!

The word *fear* means flight, or to run away from.[2] So if we translate it a little differently, we see that God was saying, "Joshua, when you **feel** fear, don't run!"

---

[2]Vine, Vol. II, p. 84.

Do you see it? God is saying, "When you **feel** fear, stand your ground, knowing that I am with you. Keep obeying Me and doing what I have told you to do!" That's much different than God saying, "Don't you ever **feel** fear! And if you do, you're a big coward!"

What are some of the physical reactions produced by fear? They are shakiness, heart palpitations, dry mouth and sweat. I cannot find anywhere in the Bible where God says, "Joyce Meyer, sweat not, shake not, tremble not! Thy heart must not palpitate when you are in new or difficult situations!"

Have you found that a spirit of fear tries to hold you in bondage when you encounter something new? When you try to gain freedom in your life, a spirit of fear will attempt to hold you in bondage. When God's day comes for you to be free, it's time to face the person or the situation that you are afraid of. It's time for you to walk up to people and talk to them, even if you are afraid. It's time to begin believing differently about yourself. Fear will try to keep you in bondage. The only way you can get on the other side of it is to dig both heels in, set your face like a flint and say, "I know I've heard from God, and I'm going forward!"

How Will People Think and React?

When we talk about the fear of man, what are we really afraid of? We are afraid of what people are going to think! Think about this: **what can another person's thoughts do to us?** Yet how many times do we bow our knees to the enemy simply on the basis of what someone else will think. Most of the time we never really know what others think, but the root of rejection will always make you think the worst.

We allow the devil to say, "What will they think of you if you do that? If you step out, and try that, and fail — what will everybody think? They'll think you didn't hear from God! They'll think you are a failure. They'll think this...they'll think that...they'll think something else." Why should we let the thoughts of others run our lives? If they have a problem, they're going to think what they want to about us no matter what we do!

The fear of man is a fear of what others will think, but it's also the fear of what others will say and do. I think we are also afraid of what people won't say or do! If I do something, and you don't like it, then you'll reject me; and I won't have your relationship and your friendship anymore. You won't talk to me and pay attention to me anymore. Then I'll have that pain of rejection to deal with.

I will prove to you with several Scriptures that Satan uses the fear of rejection to keep people out of the will of God. Let's look at what Paul said in Galatians 1:10: *Now am I trying to win the favor of men, or of God? Do I seek to please men? If I were still seeking popularity with men, I should not be a bond servant of Christ (the Messiah).*

We really like to be popular, don't we? I was never very popular in school, but I wanted all of my children to be popular. That didn't work out either! Sometimes we want things for all the wrong reasons. I wanted my daughters to be homecoming queens and cheerleaders and my sons to be "Prince Charmings" and football quarterbacks. It grieved me that they didn't really have lots of friends and dates. But one day the Lord showed me, "You want that for them because you never had it. I am keeping them out of trouble because I have a plan for their lives!"

Sometimes, when young people are popular, the peer pressure to maintain all those relationships ends up drawing them off in the wrong direction. If God had answered my prayers for my children to be the most popular students in school, things might have turned out badly. But now all of our children are serving the Lord, and they work in this ministry. The three older ones are married to Christians, and I know God has a good, godly woman set aside for our son still in school. What would have happened if God had answered my prayers for them to be popular? Let's desire popularity with God above popularity with people.

Don't be too sad if you don't have twenty-five people ringing your phone off the hook and beating down your door all the time. Seek God and let Him bring the right people into your life. Because once you get into relationships, you must maintain them; and maintaining relationships with the "popular" people can sometimes cause a lot of pressure.

Years ago before I was in ministry, I belonged to a church organization. There was a group of people I wanted to be "in" with. I worked and connived...worked and manipulated...did favors for and impressed people...until I got into that group. But I discovered that when a person gets into relationships by those methods, the only way to stay there is by letting those people control you!

Do you know what happened? When I received the baptism in the Holy Spirit and God called me to preach — when I started believing the things I now believe and started pressing forward — that group of people came to me and said, "If you are going to believe the things you say you believe, we can no longer have anything to do with you! It's us...or that!" These people were Christians! Don't think the enemy won't use your best friends to try to drag you away from the will of God! That's why you need to know in your heart what God is saying to you.

The Bible says Jesus made Himself of no reputation, and then the power of God was given to Him (see Philippians 2:7-11, KJV). If we're concerned about our reputation, we might as well hang it up! If the goal is to keep our good reputation — if we are still trying to be popular — there is a door open to the devil. All he has to do is arrange for a little rejection, and we fall apart!

Pressing On Is No Popularity Contest!

Do you realize what Paul was saying in Galatians 1:10? He was saying, "If I wanted to be popular with people, I wouldn't be serving God!" Do you know how many people there are who won't go on with what God is leading them to do with their lives because they know they would lose their popularity with people?

Every single time God has been ready to bring this ministry up another level, Satan has launched a major attack of rejection against me. Each time it has come through the people who were the closest to me at the time. Oh, don't think the enemy will pick someone you don't care anything about! The people who are close to you will let you know, "If you don't do it like we would do it, then we're going to have to look at you as very strange and unusual!"

People who have a root of rejection in their lives will bow their knee to that type of pressure and not even realize they are doing it. Whatever it takes to keep people happy...whatever it takes to keep people liking us, smiling at us and saying, "Good girl! Good boy!" that's what people with the root of rejection will find themselves doing.

I'm not teaching rebellion. I'm not teaching that you should go out and do your own thing all the time. That's not what I'm talking about. If you have someone properly in authority over you, listen to their wisdom. What I am talking about is people running your life who don't have any business doing it. Sometimes even people who are in authority over you can get into manipulation and control. But if they are exercising godly authority over you, they will help you find the perfect will of God for your life. They will not use that authority to increase their own happiness.

Now look at John 12:42 — *And yet [in spite of all this] many even of the leading men (the authorities and the nobles) believed and trusted in Him. But because of the Pharisees they did not confess it, for fear that [if they should acknowledge Him] they would be expelled from the synagogue.*

I was put out of the church I attended when I received the baptism in the Holy Spirit and God called me to preach. The leadership asked me to leave. It was hard for me because my whole life had been wrapped up in that church. After all, I had worked hard to get in with that group of people! You should have seen the way I worked to get an eldership for my husband! I wanted my husband to be an important person!

People who don't base their worth in Christ are constantly looking for something to make them feel important. They must have all the right friends. Their friends must be in positions of authority to make them feel important. So they connive and manipulate and do all kinds of things to get themselves into those positions.

But if you think it's hard to get into those lofty positions, wait until you see how hard it is to stay there!

Verse 43 says, *For they loved the approval and the praise and the glory that come from men [instead of and] more than the glory that comes from God. [They valued their credit with men more than their credit with God.]* Isn't that an awesome Scripture?

Decide To Be a God-Pleaser!

At all costs, we must decide to please God — not men. Even if it costs our reputation and our friends, we must decide to please God. If it costs us our friends, God will replace them. Dave and I have some of the most precious friends now! These are people who work for us, love us and hold up our hands in prayer. They pray for us and intercede for us when we're out on the road preaching. We know now what real friends are. Friends are not people who come to you and say, "If you don't do it my way, you're out!" That's somebody who wants to control and manipulate you!

The people I now have as friends are helping me to be all I can be in Christ. They are true friends — friends who are not jealous of me. They help me go forward. They don't try to hold me back so they can be out in front.

Sometimes people do you a favor when they lay it on the line and say, "You'd better please me, or you're out!" At least then you know what you're dealing with. But many times, control is behind the scenes, maybe something as subtle as a disapproving look. That disapproving look may cause us to totally change our minds and go in another direction.

I'm going to work with God to identify these things in my own life because I want to be free! And I want to say again, "I am not rebellious!" I submit to my husband's authority and come under the authority of my local pastor. If he came to Dave and me and said, "I think you two are mistaken in what you are planning to do," we would go back to prayer and seek God again.

Let me repeat: You need to come under the right, godly authority. I am not teaching rebellion. Sometimes it's difficult to teach on the subject of control, manipulation and the fear of man because some people take it the wrong way.

I'm talking about knowing what God is saying to you and being willing to go through whatever it takes to see the fullness of God's will in your life. I can promise you though that there are more people who are kept out of the will of God through the fear of man than people who will ever press through the attack of the enemy and get into the full will of God.

God's people desperately need to be obedient. Paul said if you're going to be a man-pleaser, you won't serve Jesus Christ. You won't be His bond servant (see Galatians 1:10). A bond servant is someone who says, "Okay, Jesus, I'm chained to You by my own choice. I want to do whatever

You want me to do no matter what it costs me. I'm Yours! Have Your way in my life!"

When I made the decision to be the bond servant of Jesus, I lost my friends. Some of my family members got mad at me. I felt like an outcast for a long time. But I'm so happy now that I can hardly stand it.

Before I received the baptism in the Holy Spirit, I was miserable! I had worked so hard to have the right group of friends and made sure that Dave was an elder in the church. There wasn't a party that the Meyers weren't invited to! And if someone tried to give a party that we weren't invited to, I would work around and make sure we received an invitation!

Do you remember ever being offended, hurt and bothered because somebody was doing something and you weren't invited? Did it make you feel rejected and worthless?

You can be free! Trust God that, if you are supposed to be there, He can get you invited. If not, be happy in Him.

9

Manipulation and Control

Webster's definition of *manipulation* is managing or influencing shrewdly or deviously; controlling or tampering with by skilled use for personal gain.

To control somebody is sin. It is a type of witchcraft! I'm not saying that, if you control others, you are a witch or you are possessed. But control is a witchcraft principle. Satan operates in manipulation and control.

God wants to lead and guide you. God will control you only if you continually give Him permission to do so. Each time God says to me, "Joyce, I want you to do this," I say, "Lord, I agree with You. Whatever You want, God, that is what I want. I give myself to You in this area. I want it if You want it." But God will not force you if you don't give your consent.

On the other hand, the devil doesn't care how he controls you. All he wants is to get his way. He will control you through demon powers coming against your mind. He will do it by using other people — maybe even those who love you and don't even know they are being used. But because you don't stand up to them, they just continue to control you! The person doing the controlling just figures that, because you won't stand up to him, you want things to continue on just the way they are!

If you let a relationship go on like that for a long period of time, the person doing the controlling gets used to it. Because the relationship has been formed that way, when you decide to come out of it, it's war! You have established something the controller doesn't want to give up, so now you have to stand your ground. If you have been in bondage to someone's control for a long time, and now want to gain your freedom, you had better be ready to stand your ground because the devil will have a fit!

Listen to the definition of *control*. It means to direct, influence, restrain, regulate, curb, exercise authority over or try to prevent. It also means to check by duplicate register. When I read that, I saw something powerful! To check by duplicate register means to keep two separate sets of books!

For example, if I was going shopping with a friend and said to her, "Now, I'm going to be buying a lot of things today, and I want to keep track of my money. So I'll write down everything I spend, and I want you to make a duplicate listing. Then we'll compare our registers at the end of the shopping trip just to make sure that I've kept a proper record of my spending." My friend would be keeping a duplicate register. If I checked with her at the end of the shopping trip to see if she had a certain figure written down, and she didn't have it; or if she had an entry that I didn't have, then I would know that something was wrong.

One of my daughters often travels with Dave and me when we minister, so she is with me a lot when I shop. Because she wears the same size clothes I wear, she gets many of my clothes when I'm finished with them. So she has a pretty strong opinion about what I buy.

Sometimes when we're out shopping, I'll try something on and ask her opinion. She will say, "Oh, yuck! No! You don't want to buy that, Mother!" Often I would hang the outfit back on the rack and look for something else. Then I would show her the next outfit I picked, and she'd say, "Oh, no! I don't like that!" And again, I would put the outfit back on the rack.

But when I started teaching this message on rejection, God showed me what was really happening. Because of the way I was raised — being abused by my father who had a strong, domineering, controlling, manipulative personality — I naturally had a real strong root of rejection in my life. If my father wanted to eat chicken, everybody ate chicken. If my father didn't want vegetables, nobody ate vegetables. He controlled everything that went on in the household. He was the kind of person who got angry and blew up a lot. So I spent most of my time just trying to keep him "fixed." I spent most of my time trying to keep from having to face that fear, rejection and displeasure.

We end up living our lives that way without even realizing what we're doing. It doesn't take the devil to totally control us because he can easily use another person to do it for him — a person who doesn't even have any ill intent on his mind. My daughter was not trying to control me. She was giving her opinion. I was letting her opinion control me because of the fear of rejection.

There are times when the devil will attempt to control you through a really controlling person, which is another problem. I'm not saying that the devil won't make arrangements to place those people in your life, because he will!

Many times those who have a terrible fear of rejection will marry someone who is strong-willed. I believe God puts them together. Do you know why? Because you'll never get over the fear of man if you're not forced to confront it and face it. If you are always looking for someone who won't reject you and you're always saying, "Don't do that to me! Don't do that to me," what you are really saying is, "I don't want to confront the problem. I don't want to deal with it anymore, so I'll just be around these meek, sweet, kind, loving people who will never give me a problem about anything!" But it won't work! Sooner or later in order to get on the other side of that fear, you are going to have to stand up to somebody. Maybe it will be a boss, a friend, a spouse or a child. Many people who have a root of rejection have strong-willed children; and unless they deal with their own fears, their children will control them!

I had a terrible fear of displeasing others and making people angry, so I always tried to keep everybody "fixed." I just wanted to keep everybody happy. I didn't want anybody to be disappointed with me. I tried so hard to be perfect and live my life in such a way that nobody would ever find anything wrong with me, then they wouldn't reject me; and I wouldn't have to experience all that pain.

Receiving this teaching from God was a real eye-opener for me. When I realized the truth, I began to take the knowledge along on my shopping trips with my daughter. I realized that she really didn't care what I bought. She is a very good and submissive daughter; and all I would have had to say to her was, "Well, I like this outfit so I'm going to buy it!" And she would have said, "Okay!" And that would have been the end of it. She was giving me her opinion, but my own fear of not pleasing people caused me to be led by her opinion instead of my own heart.

Now, the flip side of this is that sometimes I'll be out shopping with her, and I'll pick up something and not really know whether it would look good on me. So I'll ask, "Do you like this?" And sometimes she says, "No, I don't really like that." This is sort of a confirmation to me that I really wouldn't like it anyway. So again, there should be a balance. You shouldn't get obnoxious with this and start telling everyone around you, "Don't try to tell me what to do! I am doing what I want to, and it's none of your business!"

Maintain Proper Balance

I've learned that you've got to have balance. Without balance, we hear a message that we like and swing all the way over to one side...then we hear another message and swing all the way over to the other side. What we are doing is moving from being out of balance in one direction to being out of balance in another direction! We never manage to get into balance. I believe strongly in maintaining proper balance in our lives. That's why I stress that I am not teaching rebellion. I am not saying we should never listen to the opinions of others or that we should never try to please people. Sure, we want to keep people happy if we can.

Sometimes I do things just to make my husband happy because I love him. But if I did these things out of manipulation and control — hating what I was doing, feeling it was not God's will and being secretly resentful — I would be disobeying God. If I were trying to please Dave but had this secret war going on inside me, it would cause major trouble eventually in my life and in my marriage.

For much of my life, I allowed others to keep a duplicate register for me. In other words, I would start to do something, and I would immediately look around for that approving look. I was secretly saying, "Is it okay?" It's not wrong to give that approving look to someone or to get an approving look occasionally. But it is wrong when you start to fall apart if you don't get it.

I challenge you to start standing up to some of the things you have been bowing your knee to, because bowing your knee makes you unhappy unless you are bowing it in worship to God. Romans 8:2 says, *For the law of the Spirit of life [which is] in Christ Jesus [the law of our new being] has freed me from the law of sin and death.* I had to meditate on that Scripture for many years before I understood it. Do you know what Romans 8:2 says to me? If I let your opinion become law to me, then I am operating under the law of sin and death. And that is sin to me because I am not following the Spirit. Sin produces death in me. I don't mean that I will lay down and die, but I will suffer the things associated with death. It will kill my joy. *The thief comes only in order to steal and kill and destroy.* But Jesus said, *I came that* [you] *may have and enjoy life...* (John 10:10).

The law of the Spirit of life in Christ Jesus has set me free from the law of sin and death! I am now free to follow the leading of the Holy Spirit.

Helping Someone With a Root of Rejection

If you are married to someone, involved with someone, have a child in your home or work with someone who has a root of rejection, how can you help them move toward freedom? When you love God, you want to help others come out from under the bondage of the root of rejection. What can you do?

You certainly cannot spend all your life just tiptoeing around them because that will put you in bondage. But you can exhort, edify and encourage them. When they do something well, don't ignore it. Praise them, because they need a lot of encouragement. If they do something mostly right (and a little bit wrong), don't pick on what they did wrong and ignore what they did right. As you continue to give them praise, you will find that, after a time, they won't need it as often. If you are in authority over this person and have to correct him, use Galatians 6:1 as your guideline:

Brethren, if any person is overtaken in misconduct or sin of any sort, you who are spiritual [who are responsive to and controlled by the Spirit] should set him right and restore and reinstate him, without any sense of superiority and with all gentleness, keeping an attentive eye on yourself, lest you should be tempted also.

Don't correct with an air of superiority — do it with all gentleness and humility.

Because God has given me a strong personality, I present myself in a very straightforward manner. But I have had to learn to be kind, gentle and tender to people who are afraid of my type of personality. Because I'm in authority much of the time, sometimes I have to correct people. When I do, I usually tell them about something I did wrong, and how I overcame it. We have all done things that were wrong, and they need to know that they are not in a class by themselves. I tell them, "You're great. You're a wonderful person. I don't want this to tear you apart or make you feel that you're no good."

You see, we can't draw back from correcting people just because they have a root of rejection. But we can approach them in love, and be careful never to take advantage of them by playing on their weaknesses. Keeping a proper balance is very important, and God has all the answers.

Another thing you can do for those with the root of rejection is to help them to make their own decisions and respect their opinions, even if they are not like yours. You can help them hear from God.

People with this problem tend to come to you every time you turn around, asking, "Well, what do you think I should do?" Say to them, "Well, I think you should hear from God, and I believe you can!"

If they ask again what you think they should do, then say, "Well, you tell me what you think God is saying, and then I'll tell you what I think!" If they say, "Well, I think God is saying this...and this...and this," most of the time it will be right for them. It may not be exactly what you would do; but you can encourage them and say, "Well, I probably wouldn't do it that way, but I think that's great for you! You're an individual and you can hear from God and be led by Him!"

You see, there are many ways to help a person who has a root of rejection. God will lead you by His Spirit if your desire is to help.

Resisting the Temptation To Be a Controller

I cannot finish this book without saying a few things to those of you who may be trying to control someone else. Why do people try to control others? Fear of being hurt is one reason. I had been hurt so much in my life that I figured if I stayed in control of everything that went on, then nobody could hurt me. I actually operated in both sides of this problem. Because of the fear of rejection, I would often allow others to control me. And because of the fear of being hurt, I would try to control them. I was very mixed up and confused; and only God's mercy, grace, and the power and instruction of His Word could have delivered me.

It is easy to want to be free of allowing others to control you. But it is a little harder to give up controlling someone else if you have fallen into that trap. People who are controllers and manipulators are troubled, insecure people. They may appear to be strong, but actually they live in great fear. People who are truly strong are able to let others be free. I believe that many controllers feel so insecure about themselves and all their decisions that it helps them feel better about themselves if they can get everyone else doing the same thing they are doing.

In addition to fear and insecurity being the root of control, we also should uncover that the devil seeks to work on people with strong personalities. There may not be anything wrong with these people except that they were born for leadership and have strong personalities. They are gifted for keeping things going in the right direction, for motivating and for moving people along. This is all fine, except Satan delights in deceiving us and even taking our greatest God-given strengths and trying to use them against us and everyone else. He does it by getting us out of balance.

I not only had the problems from being abused; but I also have a God-given strong personality. God has anointed me for leadership. However, I had to learn the difference between leadership, control, and manipulation. I had to learn to lead people where God wanted them to go, and where they were willing to go, and not where "I" wanted them to go and into what "I" wanted them to do. Part of my problem stemmed from the fears and insecurities in my life due to abuse and rejection, but part of it was just my own personality.

Controlling people and everything around you can just be a bad habit that needs to be confronted and broken. Whatever the case may be, it needs to be dealt with. IT IS NOT GOD'S WILL FOR PEOPLE TO CONTROL OTHER PEOPLE! I had to learn that it was sin and not at all pleasing to God for me to control and manipulate others or to coerce them into doing things my way.

If you have fallen prey to allowing these controlling spirits to operate through you, I am encouraging you to begin immediately to set people free and to resist the temptation these spirits bring.

When a person has been controlled or is the controller, the spirits involved will put up a fight; but your desire to operate in holiness and God's ways will prevail. Resist the devil with The Word, The Name and The Blood. The Word of God has power in it, and it is our two-edged Sword with which we fight the enemy. The name of Jesus has all power invested in it. In His name, we pray and make our petition to God, the Father; and we steadfastly resist the enemy in the wonderful name of Jesus. There is power in the blood of the Lamb. We can apply the blood to ourselves and situations by faith, and experience deliverance. Revelation 12:11 says, *And they have overcome (conquered) him by means of the blood of the Lamb and by the utterance of their testimony....*

You were never intended to be controlled or to be a controller. Both bring misery. Not only is a person in bondage who allows others to control him but also the individual who needs to be in control. Controlling other people's lives is hard work. I feel now that I have enough to do to cooperate with God concerning my involvement with other people. I don't want to run anyone else's life. I don't want to mind anyone else's business. I have enough of my own to take care of.

If any of these areas are out of balance in your life, they need to be reconciled. That means to get things back to the way they should have been before Satan's deception got involved. A really great Scripture that I want to leave with you is Colossians 1:20: *And God purposed that through (by the service, the intervention of) Him [the Son] all things should be completely reconciled back to Himself, whether on earth or in heaven, as through Him, [the Father] made peace by means of the blood of His cross.*

All of the areas of your life that are out of order can be reconciled through Jesus and the work that He has done on the cross. Begin to believe it! Don't settle for bondage, but be determined to be free!

Conclusion

You can be free from the root of rejection!

Let's look at a few more Scriptures. Romans 12:2 says: *Do not be conformed to this world (this age), [fashioned after and adapted to its external, superficial customs], but be transformed (changed) by the [entire] renewal of your mind [by its new ideals and its new attitude], so that you may prove [for yourselves] what is the good and acceptable and perfect will of God, even the thing which is good and acceptable and perfect [in His sight for you].*

I've studied Romans 12:2, and basically what it's saying is: If you want Jesus to transform you and work in you from the inside to produce results on the outside, then you will have to make a decision not to be conformed to the world's idea of what you ought to be. It's either transformation or conformation.

Romans 7:6: *But now we are discharged from the Law and have terminated all intercourse with it, having died to what once restrained and held us captive....*

Romans 8:4,14,15: *So that the righteous and just requirement of the Law might be fully met in us who live and move not in the ways of the flesh but in the ways of the Spirit [our lives governed not by the standards and according to the dictates of the flesh, but controlled by the Holy Spirit]. For all who are led by the Spirit of God are sons of God. For [the Spirit which] you have now received [is] not a spirit of slavery to put you once more in bondage to fear, but you have received the Spirit of adoption [the Spirit producing sonship] in [the bliss of] which we cry, Abba (Father)! Father!*

Galatians 5:16,17: *But I say, walk and live [habitually] in the [Holy] Spirit [responsive to and controlled and guided by the*

Spirit]; then you will certainly not gratify the cravings and desires of the flesh (of human nature without God). For the desires of the flesh are opposed to the [Holy] Spirit, and the [desires of the] Spirit are opposed to the flesh (godless human nature); for these are antagonistic to each other [continually withstanding and in conflict with each other], so that you are not free but are prevented from doing what you desire to do.

Galatians 5:1: In [this] freedom Christ has made us free [and completely liberated us]; stand fast then, and do not be hampered and held ensnared and submit again to a yoke of slavery [which you have once put off].

Are you ready to stand fast in the freedom God has provided for you?

The first step toward freedom from the root of rejection is knowing Jesus Christ as your personal Savior. In my journey toward my own healing, I have encountered all types of "quick-fix" methods in today's hurting world. Yet I have discovered that the only lasting cure for the root of rejection is a relationship with Jesus Christ. He took your rejection upon Himself. His death and resurrection purchased your freedom and mine from the pain and behavior patterns produced by a lifetime of rejection.

If you have not made Jesus Christ your Savior, will you pray with me now?

"Jesus, I come to you a sinner. I repent of all my sins and ask You to forgive me and cleanse me by Your blood. I now make You the Lord of my life. I choose to forgive those who have hurt and rejected me. Heal me of the root of rejection. Fill me with the Holy Spirit because today I choose to allow You to do this inner work in me that will produce results on the outside for all the world to see. I choose to be transformed by Your power and Your love — not to conform to man's opinions and ideas of who and what I should be.

"Jesus, I pray that You will forgive me for any manipulative, controlling behavior that I have ever engaged in. Help me to stop manipulating and controlling others. Set me free from the fear of man. Help me to be a God-pleaser, not a man-pleaser. Teach me how to live as a victorious Christian. Reveal Your love to me and help me to truly understand that I have been accepted in the Beloved. I pray this prayer in faith, expecting life-changing results, in Jesus' name. Amen."

If you prayed this prayer, I'd like to hear from you! Please write me at:

Joyce Meyer Ministries
P. O. Box 655 • Fenton, Missouri 63026
or call: (636) 349-0303
Internet Address: www.joycemeyer.org

Please include your testimony or help received from this book when you write. Your prayer requests are welcome.

To contact the author in Canada, please write:
Joyce Meyer Ministries Canada, Inc.
Lambeth Box 1300 • London, ON N6P 1T5
or call: (636) 349-0303

In Australia, please write:
Joyce Meyer Ministries-Australia • Locked Bag 77
Mansfield Delivery Centre • Queensland 4122
or call: 07 3349 1200

In England, please write:
Joyce Meyer Ministries
P. O. Box 1549 • Windsor • SL4 1GT
or call: (0) 1753-831102

About the Author

Joyce Meyer has been teaching the Word of God since 1976 and in full-time ministry since 1980. She is the bestselling author of more than fifty inspirational books, including *How to Hear from God, Knowing God Intimately,* and *Battlefield of the Mind*. She has also released thousands of teaching cassettes and a complete video library. Joyce's *Enjoying Everyday Life* radio and television programs are broadcast around the world, and she travels extensively conducting conferences. Joyce and her husband, Dave, are the parents of four grown children and make their home in St. Louis, Missouri.

Books By Joyce Meyer

Seven Things That Steal Your Joy
How To Hear From God
Starting Your Day Right
Beauty For Ashes Revised Edition
Knowing God Intimately
The Power Of Forgiveness
The Power Of Determination
The Power Of Being Positive
The Secrets Of Spiritual Power
The Battle Belongs To The Lord
Secrets To Exceptional Living
Eight Ways To Keep The Devil Under Your Feet
Teenagers Are People Too!
Filled With The Spirit
Celebration Of Simplicity
The Joy Of Believing Prayer
Never Lose Heart
Being The Person God Made You To Be
A Leader In The Making
"Good Morning, This Is God!" Gift Book
Jesus—Name Above All Names
"Good Morning, This Is God!" Daily Calendar
Help Me—I'm Married!
Reduce Me To Love
Be Healed In Jesus' Name
How To Succeed At Being Yourself
Eat And Stay Thin
Weary Warriors, Fainting Saints
Life In The Word Journal
Life In The Word Devotional
Be Anxious For Nothing
Be Anxious For Nothing Study Guide
Straight Talk On Loneliness